EAT SKINNY, BE SKINNY

EAT SKINNY, BE SKINNY

Delicious Recipes Under 300 Calories

CLAIRE GALLAM, CREATOR OF NUTRITIONFOR.US

SKYHORSE PUBLISHING

Skyhorse Publishing books may be purchased in bulk at special discounts for sales promotion, corporate gifts, fund-raising, or educational purposes. Special editions can also be created to specifications. For details, contact the Special Sales Department, Skyhorse Publishing, 307 West 36th Street, 11th Floor, New York, NY 10018 or info@skyhorsepublishing.com.

Skyhorse® and Skyhorse Publishing® are registered trademarks of Skyhorse Publishing, Inc. ®, a Delaware corporation.

www.skyhorsepublishing.com

10 9 8 7 6 5 4 3 2 1

Library of Congress Cataloging-in-Publication Data is available on file.

Cover design by David Ter-Avanesyan
Cover photo by Shutterstock

ISBN: 978-1-5107-6505-4
eBook ISBN: 978-1-62914-102-2

Printed in China

The following recipes were originally developed for SheKnows.com: Fluffy French Crepes, 20; Blackberry Lemonade, 124; Homemade Whole Wheat Tortellini, 224; Smashed Strawberry & Blueberry Bellini, 142; Fresh Strawberry & Shrimp Salad with Strawberry Vinaigrette, 198; Sweet Potato Gnocchi, 228; Roasted Strawberry Ice Cream, 264.

This book is dedicated first and foremost to my family, the ones who have seen me at my worst and my best and who have always believed in me. To my mom, for not only teaching me to cook, but for showing me the love behind it. To my dad, for never giving up on me and supporting me. To my brothers, for being my first taste testers. To my twin, Liz, for always being right by my side offering wise words of wisdom and encouragement. To my best friend Emily who knew I could do this even when I didn't think I could. And most importantly, to my husband, without whom, I know I wouldn't have been able to do any of this. I love you all.

TABLE OF CONTENTS

INTRODUCTION

WHERE IT ALL BEGAN AND THE STORY OF THE DRAMATIC, "REALISTIC" GIRL BEHIND IT.

Growing up, I always knew I was different. I dreamt about food the way the other kids dreamt about new toys and vacations to Disney World. Food was on my mind from when I woke up to when I went to bed. When you grow up with a mother who is an incredibly talented cook and baker, one who was always baking cookies and whipping up creamy mashed potatoes, food becomes a huge part of who you are, not just something you eat for nourishment. I actually remember the first recipe I made myself when I was in 3rd grade. My brothers, my cousin Curt, my Dad, and I were in the basement playing a video game on the computer. Bored from the game, I decided I wanted to make a cake. I went into the pantry and mixed flour, unsweetened cocoa powder, a ton of cinnamon and some eggs together. I added some milk and then poured the mixture into a cake pan. I turned the oven on and slid the cake in. Of course, without baking soda, baking powder, and the right measurements, well, the cake didn't rise. It turned out hard as a rock with WAY too much cinnamon. My cousin tried it and spit it right out. Even though it was a major fail, I remember how excited I felt as I waited for the oven to ding so I could see my creation. I may not have been born with the talent of a chef, but I knew I loved more than just eating food, I loved creating it.

My love for food hasn't always had a happy ending. I was the biggest girl in my class from first grade to 7th grade. I had to wear a women's size 8 when the rest of my classmates were still in kids' sizes. I loathed wearing a bathing suit next to my skinny cousins. I never felt like I fit in. I was always the fat girl. The one with the thunder thighs. I remember one summer my cousins were on a golf cart and I hopped on the back. They turned and said, "I don't think you can ride with us. It's too heavy now." Instead of crying, I ate. I went inside our family's cottage and found solace in a package of cookies or a pint of ice cream. As much joy food brought me, it brought equal amounts of pain. I hated what I looked like; I hated how food made me feel. It wasn't until age fourteen that I discovered I could actually do something about the way I felt.

I joined the middle school swim team when I entered 7th grade. I was overweight, unhappy, and in desperate need of exercise. I always felt confident in the water and swimming was always a release for me, so I happily joined. A few weeks into the season, my coach asked us to start keeping a food journal. He explained how the way we ate dramatically affected the way we swam. Jealous of how fast some of my teammates were, I took this undertaking very seriously.

I wrote down everything I ate, even the gum I chewed and the diet soda I drank. The night before we had to turn our first week's entries in, I looked at what I had eaten that week. I don't think I've ever felt so ashamed. Boxes of macaroni and cheese, packets of Kool-Aid and double servings of cake. I was so embarrassed, I forgot it at home on purpose so I wouldn't have to compare notes with my skinny teammates or my judgmental coach. That next week I worked my butt off to eat better. And when I turned my journal in after my week of healthy eating, I had not only impressed my coach, but lost a few pounds too. When the season ended a few months later, I had lost over twenty-five pounds and was the thinnest I had ever been. For the first time in my life, I felt good about myself. I felt pretty. I finally understood the importance of healthy eating.

Although I still indulged in plenty of decadent meals, that was a very defining moment in my life. It was when I fell in love with healthy food and nutrition. When I entered college, I even took a few classes in nutrition so I could better understand it. Even though I quickly learned that science wasn't my forte, the study of nutrition always fascinated me. It was that interest that inspired me to start my blog in November of 2009. The funny thing about that was I started it as a solely nutrition blog, one that had nothing to do with cooking or recipe development. To be honest, I didn't really fall in love with cooking until a few months later.

The first recipe on my blog that I actually photographed (with an iPhone 3S), developed, and posted was a salmon steak with salsa. I only got about two comments (from my childhood friends) but I remember how much fun I had doing it. I finally understood the joy, the passion and the romance my mom felt when she made meals for us every night. From that moment on, I threw everything I had into cooking. A blog that originally began as a distraction from the job I hated and a way to understand more about nutrition turned into my dream come true, a database of healthy recipes that brought joy and purpose to my life.

Many people have those defining moments in their lives where something happened that completely changed who they were and where they were going. For me, that was the day I started my blog. My blog brought me back to life. It reignited my passion for food and my dream of writing. It gave me a reason to wake up and a reason to live. My blog introduced me to my dream job (which I'm doing now) as a recipe developer and travel writer. And my blog is what pushed me to apply to culinary school in Paris, France. It's what really showed me that food has always been and will always be my first and my one true love.

WHAT CAN YOU FIND IN THIS BOOK?

You'll find everything you need and more in *Eat Skinny, Be Skinny*! This cookbook has 100 incredibly delicious recipes all under 300 calories and covers meals for everyday as well as big occasions like holidays and parties. This cookbook is for everyone, from beginning cooks to experienced chefs. No matter what your tastes, your preferences or your likes/dislikes, there's a recipe for you. There are recipes for vegans, vegetarians, carnivores, pescatarians, and people with gluten allergies and sensitivities. There are recipes for people trying to lose weight or those trying to maintain. *Eat Skinny, Be Skinny* has recipes for those who love to bake and for those who love to cook. This book is for people, like me, who love eating but also love being healthy, happy, and in shape. For those who, like me, have struggled with their weight and want to take charge of how they look and feel. For those who want a skinny lifestyle while still enjoying their favorite foods, like cinnamon rolls, fluffy cakes and crock pot casseroles. Most importantly, this is for all the women and men out there who love food and know how to enjoy a meal.

STOCKING A SKINNY KITCHEN

Many people think cooking healthfully, light, or "skinny" is hard or expensive or bland. Even though fresh, healthy ingredients are more expensive than say, boxed dinners or preservative laden ones, you can still have a fully stocked healthy kitchen for under $100. The key to staying on track with any weight loss plan or healthy lifestyle is having good-for-you, satisfying snacks and ingredients on hand in your kitchen. Many emails I get from readers trying to lose weight, maintain their weight, or eat better ask what I have in my pantry. Although it's often under stocked and a little messier than I'd like, you can be sure to find one of each of these in my fridge, pantry, or baking cabinet.

PANTRY:

Staples:

I love having these essentials like whole-wheat noodles, chia seeds, and sweet potatoes, because they are easy to prepare when I'm in a rush. Plus, many of them are filled with healthy antioxidants, whole grains, and fiber, so they instantly boost the nutritional value of whatever I add them to.

- Whole wheat pastas like spaghetti or penne
- Oats
- Quinoa
- Low-sodium diced tomatoes
- Low-sodium chicken, beef, and vegetable broth
- Peanut butter (the chunky kind)
- Brown and arborio rice
- Corn meal
- Flax seed
- Chia seeds
- Legumes like lentils, roasted peanuts, pecans, cashews, and walnuts
- Extra virgin olive oil
- Assortment of vinegars (balsamic, white wine, red wine, champagne)
- Beans (kidney, black, garbanzo, and cannellini)
- Dijon mustard
- Sweet potatoes
- Red and white russet potatoes
- Panko bread crumbs

Dry Spices:

Cooking light and healthfully often means using less fats and heavy ingredients, which means you need more innovative ways to make the dish taste great. That's why I love having these dried spices on hand. They instantly add vibrancy and flavor to a dish without adding any unnecessary fat or calories.

- Bay leaves
- Basil
- Ginger
- Garlic powder
- Italian seasoning
- Mexican seasoning
- Cajun seasoning
- Poultry seasoning
- Celery salt
- Dry mustard
- Nutmeg
- Cinnamon
- Oregano
- Crushed red pepper
- Chili powder
- Onion powder
- Paprika
- Dried cilantro leaves
- Salt
- Pepper to grind

Baking Cabinet:

I love baking. Whenever I get the chance I'm always whipping up a homemade bread or batch of low-fat cookies. These ingredients are always in my cabinet, no matter what season!

- Whole wheat flour
- All-purpose flour
- Bread flour
- Gluten-free flour
- Gluten-free biscuit mix
- Gluten-free cake mix (chocolate and vanilla, Bob's Red Mill)
- Almond meal
- Corn meal
- Baking powder
- Baking soda
- Confectioners sugar
- Food dye
- Xanthan gum

- Sweetened and unsweetened coconut
- Unsweetened applesauce (unopened)
- Brown sugar
- White sugar
- All-natural sweeteners
- Cocoa powder
- Chocolate chips (milk, bittersweet, white, butterscotch, and dark)
- Molasses
- Vanilla extract
- Gluten-free vanilla extract
- Coconut oil
- Canola oil

FRIDGE MUST-HAVES:

One of my biggest pet peeves is opening the fridge and not seeing one of these ingredients in there. One of my favorite parts about low-fat cooking is getting to use as many fresh vegetables and fruits as I'd like! Plus, as a baker and an avid coffee drinker, I can't live without milk or cream!

Dairy:

- Skim milk
- 2 percent milk
- Heavy cream
- Light cream
- Unsalted butter
- Nonfat Greek yogurt
- Unsweetened applesauce (opened)
- Eggs (organic)
- Parmesan cheese
- Fresh mozzarella
- Part-skim cheddar and mozzarella cheese
- Vegan style shreds

Meats:

- Low-sodium bacon
- Ground turkey
- Gimme Lean vegetarian substitute
- Tofu
- Chicken sausage
- Steak

Produce:

- Carrots
- Celery
- Garlic
- Lemons
- Limes
- Onions (red and yellow)
- Baby arugula
- Mushrooms (baby bella)
- Tomatoes
- Peaches
- Apples
- Blueberries
- Raspberries
- Strawberries
- Shallots
- Sweet peppers
- Bell peppers
- Kale

Herbs (fresh):

- Cilantro
- Basil
- Chives
- Dill
- Rosemary
- Sage
- Thyme

Freezer Basics:

- Frozen vegetables
- Frozen fruit
- Ground turkey
- Puff pastry
- Peas
- Spinach and kale

BREAKFAST & BRUNCH

Breakfast will always remind me of my dad. My mom is an incredible cook and when I was growing up she had reign over dinnertime. Of course, there were those nights when she'd be working or tired, so dad would pick up the slack. But in my family it was always this: Mom had dinner, dad had breakfast. Every Saturday morning, almost like clockwork, my dad would be found in the kitchen, a box of Bisquick to his right and a pound of bacon to his left. And I, without being asked, would grab the mixing bowls and spoons and start stirring that chunky, delicious pancake batter. Every weekend the pancakes were different. Some days I'd throw in bananas and sometimes a ton of chocolate chips or cinnamon sugar. We'd be laughing and making a disaster of the kitchen while my older brother slept and my younger brothers ran around the house.

Breakfast has never been just a meal to me; it's been a source of some of my favorite childhood memories.

Although I wish every morning was a pancake morning in my house, I have to be realistic. Which is why I've created some healthy and delicious recipes that suit every type of morning. From those crazed Monday mornings when we're running out the door with a thermos of spilling coffee, a stained shirt, and an open mascara wand, to those relaxed Sunday mornings where we're sipping coffee lazily in our favorite cashmere throw over, there's a healthy, delicious, and easy meal you can make to start your day healthfully and happily.

FLUFFY FRENCH CREPES

French crepes are American pancake's thinner, prettier, and more sophisticated cousins. These are the brunch treat you'd bring over to your snobby neighbor's house to show her up. Unlike pancakes, they won't weigh you down with excess calories and carbohydrates. (And, unlike your snobby neighbor, they won't insult you about the state of your hydrangeas).

Serves about 4-5

Ingredients:

- 1 cup all-purpose flour
- 2 eggs
- ⅔ cup milk
- ⅓ cup water
- Dash of salt
- 2 tablespoons melted butter
- About 1 cup sliced strawberries
- Fresh whipped cream

Nutritional information per serving (about 2 crepes):

Calories: 240

Fat: 8 grams

Carbohydrates: 25 grams

Protein: 7 grams

Fiber: 4.5 grams

Directions:

1. Heavily spray a small to medium skillet with nonstick cooking spray. Heat over medium heat.
2. Mix the flour, eggs, milk, water, salt, and melted butter together with a whisk (to keep it fluffy). Pour mixture into a pitcher. Chill for about an hour to let the batter relax.
3. Carefully pour the batter into the skillet (about ¼ cup). Carefully swish the batter around so it covers the skillet. Cook for about 2 minutes or until light brown.
4. Top with whipped cream and strawberries.

CREPE TIP: Use a heavy bottomed (like copper) stainless steel plate. This will ensure the pan heats evenly and the crepes are perfectly browned on both sides. For easy pouring or to create designs with your crepes, pour the batter into a squeeze bottle.

MEXICAN BREAKFAST TACOS

If there's one thing my husband can't get enough of, it's scrambled eggs. Since I cook five days a week, he takes the initiative to make breakfast every Saturday. And what's on the menu is usually a batch of scrambled eggs and biscuits. These Mexican eggs are a take on his favorite breakfast, just with a bit more spice, peppers, and zesty cheese.

Serves about 4

Ingredients:

- 2 tablespoons extra virgin olive oil
- ½ cup chopped tomatoes
- ¼ cup chopped onion
- 1 tomatillo, husked and chopped
- ¼ cup chopped bell pepper
- 1 large jalapeño, seeded and chopped
- 4 eggs, beaten
- 1 teaspoon Mexican blend seasoning
- 3-4 teaspoons chopped cilantro
- ¼ cup shredded cheese
- 4 tablespoons black olives
- 4 soft tortillas

Nutritional information per serving (about 2 crepes):

Calories: 175.5

Fat: 13.2 grams

Carbohydrates: 5.3 grams

Protein: 8.5 grams

Fiber: 2.6 grams

Directions:

1. Heat olive oil in a medium-size skillet over medium high heat. Add onions, peppers, and jalapeño and cook until soft, about 3-4 minutes. Mix in the tomatoes, tomatillo, seasoning, and eggs.
2. Using a spatula, scramble the mixture. Cook until eggs are fluffy, about 2-3 minutes.
3. Add salt and pepper to taste. Garnish with fresh cilantro.
4. Serve eggs with tortillas and one tablespoon of cheese.

CREAMY PUMPKIN PIE OATMEAL

Yes, that's right friends, I'm totally giving you the thumbs up to have pie for breakfast. Parents, before you come after me with pitchforks and sticks, let me clarify. When I say pie, I simply mean this creamy, hearty, and slightly sweet pumpkin pie oatmeal. Served with a dab of low-fat whipped cream, each bite tastes like Thanksgiving, without all the annoying relatives asking you why you haven't had kids yet.

Serves about 4

Ingredients:

- 2 cups low-fat milk
- 2 cups water
- 2 cups old-fashioned oats (not instant)
- 1 cup canned pumpkin (not pumpkin pie mix)
- About 1 teaspoon pumpkin pie spice
- 4 tablespoons brown sugar
- 1 teaspoon vanilla or almond extract
- ¼ cup chopped walnuts
- Fresh whipped cream

Nutritional information per serving:

Calories: 308

Fat: 9.8 grams

Carbohydrates: 51.9 grams

Protein: 11.3 grams

Fiber: 4.5 grams

Directions:

1. In a medium size saucepan, heat milk, water, and oats on low heat until it simmers. Add pumpkin and spice. Bring mixture to a boil and stir for at least 5 minutes or until thick.
2. Remove from heat and stir in brown sugar, vanilla, and walnuts. Serve with fresh whipped cream and a dash of cinnamon.

CHOCOLATE PEANUT BUTTER CHIA SMOOTHIE

Weekends aside, I'm not a habitual breakfast eater. In fact, you could probably compare my weekday breakfast habits to that of Rachel Zoe ("one pot of black coffee with a straw, please"). That's why I love protein and fiber packed smoothies like this chocolate peanut butter chia seed one. I'm able to suck it through a straw and it keeps me full for hours.

Serves about 2 (about 1 cup serving size)

Ingredients:

- 3 tablespoons chia seeds
- 2 tablespoons peanut butter
- 2 frozen bananas
- 1¼ cups skim milk*
- ½ cup skim milk
- 2 tablespoons cocoa powder, unsweetened
- 1 tablespoon honey or brown sugar

*Add additional milk if too thick.

> **Nutritional information per serving:**
>
> Calories: 300
>
> Fat: 20.5 grams
>
> Carbohydrates: 30.5 grams
>
> Protein: 13.5 grams
>
> Fiber: 6.5 grams

Directions:

1. Pour all of the ingredients into a blender and pulse on low until mixture is thick and creamy. Add more milk if it's too thick for you. Pour into a cup and enjoy!

WHY I'M GAGA FOR CHIA!

1. Chia seeds are an excellent source of omega-3 fatty acids. Researchers even say it's a comparable source to that of fish. Which is great for vegans!
2. They are loaded with fiber; 25 grams (or 1⅔ tablespoons) of chia seeds has over 7 grams of soluble fiber. Fiber is good, friends, it keeps you fuller longer!
3. Chia seeds were actually used by the Mayans and Aztecs as energizing snacks. They give you a natural boost without the need for caffeine.
4. Unlike flax, chia seeds don't need to be refrigerated after opening. They stay fresh for up to a year in a pantry!

WHOLE WHEAT BANANA BREAD BARS

What my readers want me to make always surprises me. I think they want creative, unique recipes and instead, they just want the classics lightened up. Banana bread is one of the most searched recipes on my site, in fact. Instead of a loaf, I turned this classic breakfast bread into bars, making it easier to eat and snack on. Plus, with just 129 calories per bar, you can snack without worry.

Yields 12 squares

Ingredients:

- 1 large egg, room temperature
- ⅓ cup light brown sugar
- 1 teaspoon vanilla extract
- 1 teaspoon almond extract
- 3 medium bananas, ripe and mashed
- 1½ cups whole wheat flour
- 1½ teaspoons baking powder
- ¾ teaspoon apple pie spice
- ¼ cup unsweetened applesauce
- ⅓ cup chopped walnuts

Nutritional information per bar:

Calories: 129

Fat: 3 grams

Carbohydrates: 25.2 grams

Protein: 3.5 grams

Fiber: >1 gram

Directions:

1. Preheat oven to 350°F. Grease an 8 x 8 baking dish with nonstick cooking spray.
2. In a large bowl, beat the egg, brown sugar, vanilla, almond, applesauce and bananas together until smooth. Stir in the flour, baking powder, and spice together. Make a well in the center and stir in the wet mixture.
3. Mix to combine (don't overmix). Stir in nuts and pour mixture into the prepared pan. Bake for about 22 minutes or until a toothpick inserted in the middle comes out clean.

FRESH BLUEBERRY LEMON SCONES

Hi, my name is Claire and I'm 150 percent addicted to blueberries. Even though my favorite way to eat them is right from the carton, I sometimes like to bake with them too. These luscious scones pair my favorite flavor combination, blueberries and lemon, together in one perfectly moist breakfast treat.

Serves about 12

Ingredients:

- 1 cup whole wheat flour
- ¾ cup all-purpose flour
- 1 tablespoon baking powder
- 3 tablespoons brown sugar
- Dash of salt
- ¼ cup unsalted butter
- ¼ cup unsweetened applesauce
- Zest from one lemon
- 1 tablespoon lemon juice
- ½ cup low-fat buttermilk
- ¼ cup skim milk
- 1 egg, room temperature
- 1 cup fresh blueberries

Nutritional information per serving:

Calories: 95.1

Fat: 1 gram

Carbohydrates: 19.5 grams

Protein: 3.5 grams

Fiber: >1 gram

Directions:

1. Preheat oven to 400°F. In a large mixing bowl, whisk the flours, baking powder, sugar, and salt together. Set aside.
2. In another bowl, beat the egg, buttermilk, lemon juice, and skim milk together. Make a well in the center of the dry mixture and add the egg mixture, stir to combine.
3. Using a pastry cutter, cut in the butter until mixture resembles a soft sand. Stir in the applesauce with a fork until just combined (you want them to still be slightly flakey). Fold in the fresh blueberries and lemon zest.
4. Using a large spoon, scoop batter onto a baking sheet greased with nonstick cooking spray. Bake for about 13–15 minutes or until golden.

FRESH STRAWBERRY MUFFINS WITH CRUMB TOPPING

In 2012, I was lucky enough to tour a strawberry farm in Monterey, California. After stuffing my face with about two pounds of strawberries right from the field, my mind was filled with ways I could use these luscious fruits in baking. These fresh strawberry muffins were the first, and best, idea I got after that trip. The fresh chunks of berry paired with the buttery, sweet topping make for the best on the go breakfast.

Serves about 12

Ingredients:

- ⅓ cup unsweetened applesauce
- 1½ tablespoons unsalted butter, softened
- ⅔ cup brown sugar
- 1 egg, room temperature
- 1 cup all-purpose flour
- 1 cup whole wheat flour
- 2 teaspoons baking powder
- Dash of salt
- ½ cup 1 percent milk
- ½ teaspoon vanilla extract
- 1½ cups fresh strawberries, chopped

For the topping:

- About 1 teaspoon apple pie spice
- 3 tablespoons white sugar

Nutritional information per muffin:

Calories: 135

Fat: 3 grams

Carbohydrates: 29.1 grams

Protein: 4 grams

Fiber: 2 grams

Directions:

1. Preheat oven to 375°F. Line a muffin tin with paper liners and set aside.
2. In a large bowl, whisk the flours, baking powder, and salt together. In another bowl, beat the butter, applesauce, brown sugar, egg, and vanilla together with a hand mixer.
3. Alternately add the flour mixture and milk into the egg mixture, ending with the flour mixture. Stir in the chopped strawberries carefully so they don't break.
4. Fill each muffin liner two-thirds full with batter. Whisk the spice and sugar together. Sprinkle the batter with sugar and spice mixture.

STRAWBERRY TIP: Hate when your fresh strawberries start to get squishy, gross, and moldy after just a few days? Line a glass container with paper towels and place your *dry* strawberries on top (don't overcrowd, the touching of the berries will make them go bad faster). Then place another paper towel over those and seal the container. Your berries will stay fresh longer!

OATMEAL RUM RAISIN PANCAKES

Having a rough morning? Make these oatmeal rum raisin pancakes. You can't help but cheer up after a few bites of these perfect pancakes. Plus, this recipe gives you the chance to sneak some (er, a cup) rum into your coffee. When pancakes can't help, rum can.

Serves about 6 (1 pancake each)

Ingredients:

For the raisins:

- 3½ snack-size packages raisins
- 2 tablespoons brown rum (I used Brugal)
- 1 teaspoon brown sugar

For the pancakes:

- ¾ cup whole wheat flour
- ¼ cup all-purpose flour
- 2 teaspoons baking powder
- ½ teaspoon cinnamon
- 3 tablespoons sugar
- 3 tablespoons Chobani nonfat vanilla yogurt
- ½ cup plus 2½ tablespoons nonfat milk
- 1½ tablespoons brown rum*
- 1 egg, beaten

> **Nutritional information per serving (1 pancake):**
>
> Calories: 200
> Fat: 1.5 grams
> Carbohydrates: 35 grams
> Protein: 6 grams
> Fiber: 2.45 grams

*If you don't want to add rum to the pancake batter, omit the rum and add additional milk or add rum extract. Similarly, you can soak the raisins in the extract or the milk instead of rum.

Directions:

1. In a shallow bowl, mix the raisins, rum, and brown sugar together. Let sit for at least 15–20 minutes. Strain the raisins once they've soaked and discard the liquid.
2. To make the pancakes: Using a wire mesh strainer, sift the flours, baking powder, cinnamon, and sugar together in a large mixing bowl. Add the egg, milk, rum, yogurt, and rum soaked raisins. Mix to combine. Stir gently. Do not over mix; it's okay if you have a few chunks or lumps.
3. Let batter sit for 5–10 minutes.
4. Liberally spray a skillet with nonstick cooking spray and heat over medium high heat. Using an ice cream scoop, add about 2 scoops of batter into the center of the pan. Once the batter starts to bubble in the middle, flip over (about 2 minutes). Let cook an additional 2–3 minutes until golden brown on both sides.
5. Serve with syrup, whipped cream, and butter and enjoy!

VEGETARIAN BREAKFAST HASH WITH BUTTERNUT SQUASH

To my future children, I hope you come out loving the taste of squash and goat cheese because they are going to be in the base of 90 percent your meals until you're eighteen and can move out. But don't worry, darling little ones, most of those meals will also have bacon.

This vegetarian breakfast hash is the perfect breakfast to make when you're completely out of eggs and don't feel like going to the store. It's easy, it's healthy, and it doesn't require you to brush your teeth or put on mascara.

Serves about 2

Ingredients:

- ⅓ medium onion, finely chopped
- ½ yellow or red bell pepper, finely chopped
- ½ tablespoon unsalted butter
- 2 pieces of low-sodium bacon
- 1½ cups cooked diced butternut squash
- Liberal dashes of salt and pepper
- 1½ teaspoons Italian seasoning
- 1⅔ ounces soft goat cheese

> **Nutritional information per serving (about ¾–⅝ a cup):**
>
> Calories: 191
>
> Fat: 9 grams
>
> Carbohydrates: 22 grams
>
> Protein: 9.5 grams
>
> Fiber: 3 grams

Directions:

1. In a large skillet, cook bacon over medium heat until crispy. Remove from heat and place on a paper towel to absorb grease.
2. In another medium pan, melt butter over medium heat. Add onion and cook until fragrant and soft, about 2 minutes. Add pepper and cook another 3-4 minutes. Add salt, pepper, and oregano. Add in cooked squash and heat about 2 minutes longer, stirring well so the squash absorbs the seasoning and butter. Remove from heat. Season with additional salt or pepper to taste.
3. Pour vegetable mixture into 2 bowls. Sprinkle each with 1 slice of bacon and ¾ ounce of goat cheese. Garnish with additional oregano and enjoy!

QUICK SQUASH CUTTING TIP: Before roasting, peel the squash with a potato peeler and then cut off the top and bottom. To cut in half with ease, you want the bottom to be flat. Then, hold the squash on one side and cut with a sharp chef's knife right down the middle.

CARROT CAKE CINNAMON ROLLS

There isn't a day in my life where I'd rather eat a bowl of say, Grape-Nuts than a piece of cake. However, starting your day with a big slice of cake isn't exactly the way to go if you're trying to stay in shape. That's why I love these gooey, delicious carrot cake cinnamon rolls. Each bite tastes like a piece of cake but in a delicious breakfast food. Plus, you can trick your body into thinking it's a cheat day when really, one of these rolls will only set you back less than 300 calories, gooey, dripping glaze, and all!

Yields about 16 rolls

Ingredients:

For the dough:

- 1 package active dry yeast
- 1 cup warm 1 percent milk
- ½ cup brown sugar sugar
- 2 tablespoons butter, room temperature
- 2 tablespoons unsweetened applesauce
- 2 eggs
- 2½ cups bread flour
- 2½ cups whole wheat flour
- About 1½ cups shredded carrots

Nutritional information per roll:

Calories: 294.23

Fat: 6.2 grams

Carbohydrates: 52.3 grams

Protein: 8.5 grams

Fiber: 3 grams

For the filling:

- 3 tablespoons unsalted butter, softened
- ⅔ cup brown sugar
- 4½ tablespoons chopped walnuts
- 2 tablespoons pumpkin pie spice

For the icing:

- 6 ounces fat-free cream cheese
- ¾ cup powdered sugar
- About ¼ cup low-fat milk
- 1½ teaspoons vanilla
- About 2 tablespoons shredded carrots

Directions:

1. Add the yeast to the warm milk and let bubble for about 10 minutes.

2. Add the eggs, butter, unsweetened applesauce, carrots, and sugar. Beat until fully combined. Whisk the flours together in a large bowl. Add them, one cup at a time, until the dough starts to come together. Beat the dough until soft and elastic, about 6 minutes.

3. Spray a large mixing bowl with nonstick cooking spray. Roll the dough in the mixing bowl until its coated. Cover with a greased piece of saran wrap. Place in a warm spot to rise until doubled in size, about 60 minutes.

4. While the dough rises, prepare the filling by mixing all of the ingredients together in a mixing bowl.

5. Once dough has doubled, punch down. Using a rolling pin, roll the dough into a rectangle. Spread the filling over the top of the rectangle, leaving a 1-inch border around the parameter.

6. Preheat oven to 350°F. Carefully and tightly roll the dough jellyroll style so the filling doesn't spill out. Push the seams down. Using a sharp serrated knife, cut the roll into about 16 rolls. Place the rolls on a greased baking sheet and cover with a greased piece of saran wrap. Let rise for about an hour, or until doubled in size.

7. Once doubled, bake for about 20 minutes or until golden brown.

8. While the rolls bake, make the glaze by beating the cream cheese, powdered sugar, vanilla, and milk.

9. Once the rolls have cooled, drizzle with glaze and top with shredded carrots.

LIGHT BREADS & ROLLS

This portion of my book is dedicated to my husband, the resident bread-monster. When he's home and there's a loaf of homemade bread in the oven, you can bet he's pacing around the stove, anxiously waiting for it to beep so he can slice into the piping hot, soft, fluffy bread. It got to the point he was eating so much bread, he put himself on a "no bread" diet, refusing to buy loaves at the store or make his famous cinnamon bread in the bread machine. Even though he's still watching his carb intake, you better believe he threw himself into the new job of "bread and roll taste tester" when it came to finding the perfect recipes for this section.

Bread isn't just something you butter for breakfast or smudge with peanut butter for a lunchtime sandwich. Bread is bigger than that. It's a peace offering when you've gotten into a horrible fight with your brother or sister. It's a welcome to the new neighbors who just moved in. It's a beautiful accessory to your favorite soup. It's a smile through the tears after a long day at school, work, or life. Bread is at the center of so many of our meals and for me, it's at the center of so many of my favorite food memories. When it came to finding the perfect bread recipes for this book, I wanted to make sure they met three very important criteria: 1) They taste amazing, of course. 2) They are effortlessly easy and fun to make, and 3) They make you happy, relieved, excited and carefree. When you're done, I want you to remember that you may not have the rest of your life in order, but you can make an amazing loaf of whole wheat cranberry oat bread or a big batch of the perfect sweet potato rolls, and for now, that's good enough.

PRETZEL BALLS

Want to win the affections of that sexy, whispy-haired boy next door with the pickup truck and bulging biceps? Make a batch of these crispy, whole wheat pretzel balls and bring them over. After one bite, he'll be yours. I guarantee it. Also, a little red lipstick can't hurt.

Yields about 24 pretzel balls

Ingredients:

- 1 cup whole wheat flour
- 1½ cups bread flour
- 1 teaspoon sugar
- 1 package active dry yeast
- 1 cup warm water (at least 110°F)
- Dash of salt
- ½ cup warm water
- 2 tablespoons baking soda
- 2 tablespoons unsalted butter
- Salt

Nutritional information per ball:

Calories: 56.3

Fat: 1 gram

Carbohydrates: 9.8 grams

Protein: 1.8 grams

Fiber: >1 gram

Directions:

1. In the bowl of a stand mixer, add water and yeast. Let sit and bubble until foamy, about 10 minutes. Add sugar and flours and beat with a dough hook until soft and elastic, about 5 minutes.
2. Remove dough from bowl and place in a greased bowl. Top with greased saran wrap and place in a warm area. Let rise until doubled in size, about an hour.
3. Remove from the oven and punch dough down. Let rest about 5 minutes.
4. Dissolve the baking soda and warm water together. Pull 1½-inch size pieces from the rested dough. Roll into balls and place on a parchment lined baking sheet. Let rest another 10 minutes.
5. Once rested, brush each pretzel ball with baking soda mixture. Add freshly ground sea salt.
6. Preheat oven to 500°F. Bake pretzel balls for about 8–10 minutes or until golden brown.
7. Let cool for about a minute. Brush with melted butter and add additional salt to taste.

WHOLE WHEAT OAT BREAD WITH CRANBERRIES & HONEY

When I'm having a no-good, crummy day, I make homemade bread. Because homemade bread doesn't make you cry. It doesn't judge you because your bank account has $3.50 cents. It doesn't mock you because you can't fit into your size 6 jeans anymore. It doesn't talk back when you ask it to unload the dishwasher. It does exactly what you tell it to. It rises, it falls, and it kneads to soft, elastic perfection. And when it's done baking, it slices and tastes like pure happiness.

When those days come, this whole wheat oat bread with cranberries and honey is my go-to. It's hearty enough for a sandwich and has a bit of sweetness from the cranberries.

Yields 1 loaf

Ingredients:

- 1 cup water
- 1 cup 1 percent milk milk
- 2¼ teaspoons (1 packet) active dry yeast
- 2 tablespoons honey
- 1½ cups whole wheat flour
- 3 cups bread flour
- 1 cup rolled oats
- ½ cup dried cranberries
- 2 tablespoons melted butter
- 2 tablespoons unsweetened applesauce
- Dash of salt

Nutritional information per serving (about 1 slice):

Calories: 252

Fat: 2.8 grams

Carbohydrates: 49 grams

Protein: 8 grams

Fiber: 4 grams

Directions:

1. Whisk the water and milk together in a microwave safe dish. Heat for about 1 minute or until warm.
2. In the bowl of a stand mixer, add the yeast, honey, and warm milk and water. Let sit until foamy, about 10 minutes. Add the applesauce and butter and mix to combine.
3. Attach the dough hook to your mixer. Add in the flours, oats, and cranberries.
4. Continue beating for about 6–8 minutes or until dough is soft, elastic, and not sticky.

5. Grease a large bowl with nonstick cooking spray. Roll the dough ball in the oil. Cover with a greased sliced of saran wrap and let rise in a warm spot until doubled in size, about 70 minutes.

6. Once doubled, punch down. Place dough in a greased loaf pan. Cover with saran wrap and let double again for about an hour.

7. Once doubled, preheat oven to 400°F. Top with additional oats for garnish.

8. Bake bread for about 40 minutes or until golden brown.

YEAST TIP: Don't be scared of yeast! To keep the yeast alive (so your bread grows) make sure the liquid you use is 110°F. If the water is too hot, the yeast dies. If it's too cold, the yeast will go to sleep.

FRESH SWEET POTATO ROLLS

When I set out to make these sweet potato rolls, I have a "come to Jesus" moment with myself. I say "Claire, now, you know how you get with these rolls. You know you can't control yourself. You say you're going to have just one but then you end up having eight. And then you curse yourself and drink a bottle of wine to combat the guilty feelings. So, instead of that whole song and dance, let's just acknowledge that you're going to eat eight and get over it."

Yields about 8 rolls

Ingredients:

- ½ cup mashed sweet potatoes (fully mashed, no lumps)
- ½ cup heavy whipping cream
- ½ cup low-fat buttermilk
- 2 tablespoons unsalted butter, melted
- 2 tablespoons unsweetened applesauce
- 2 tablespoons brown sugar
- 1 package active dry yeast
- 1 teaspoon sea salt
- 3 cups bread flour

Nutritional information per roll:

Calories: 261

Fat: 5.8 grams

Carbohydrates: 42 grams

Protein: 7.4 grams

Fiber: 2.4 grams

Directions:

1. Preheat oven to 200°F.
2. Heat the cream and buttermilk to 110°F. Mix the milk, cream, sugar, and the yeast together and let bubble until foamy, about 10 minutes.
3. Add the butter, warm sweet potato, salt, and bread flour, 1 cup at a time or until fully mixed.
4. Turn the dough on a lightly floured surface and knead until soft, about 6 minutes. Roll dough into a ball and place in an oiled bowl. Cover with a damp towel and let rise for about an hour.
5. Once dough has doubled in size, punch down slightly. Pull apart into 8 pieces and place in an oiled muffin tin. Cover with greased plastic wrap and let rise again for about 45 minutes. Once doubled again, roll the pieces into soft balls again. Place in another greased muffin tin.
6. Preheat oven to 375°F. Bake rolls for about 20 to 25 minutes or until browned. Let them cool completely.

CRISPY WHOLE WHEAT ITALIAN HERBS AND OLIVE OIL BREAD

One of the best trips I've ever been on was in 2010 when I went to Italy with my family. Even though the sights were incredible, the people hilarious and animated, and the wine a plenty, what I most remember is how incredible the bread was dipped in the olive oil and Italian herbs. Between the six of us, we'd eat at least four loaves and probably a bottle of olive oil at every dinner. This bread has all of the flavors I loved from Italy in one delicious bite.

Yields 2 small loaves or one medium size loaf

Ingredients:

- ¾ package active dry yeast
- ½ cup warm water (110°F)
- 1 teaspoon sugar
- 1 tablespoon extra virgin olive oil + more for brushing
- ¾ cup whole wheat flour
- ¾ cup bread flour
- 1 tablespoon chopped Italian herbs
- Dash of sea salt
- Dash of freshly ground pepper

Nutritional information per serving (about 1 slice):

Calories: 101.6

Fat: 2 grams

Carbohydrates: 17.6 grams

Protein: 3.1 grams

Fiber: 1.1 grams

Directions:

1. In the bowl of a stand mixer, add the yeast, sugar, and 2 tablespoons water. Let sit until yeast foams and bubbles up about 5–6 minutes.
2. Stir in olive oil, chopped herbs, and remaining warm water. Add in the flour and stir the mixture with your dough hook until a soft dough forms..
3. Remove the dough and place on a floured surface. Knead for a few minutes until soft. Then, place back into a clean stand mixer bowl and knead with the dough hook until soft and elastic, about 8 minutes.
4. Brush another bowl with olive oil. Roll the dough into the olive oil or until greased on all sides. Cover the bowl with greased saran wrap and place in a warm area. Let rise until doubled in size, about 2 hours.
5. Brush a baking sheet with nonstick cooking spray. Punch the dough down and then roll, with floured hands. Divide into two pieces (or keep as one).
6. Fold the sides to make a square. Turn the dough over, tuck the corners so it becomes an oval shape. Cover with greased saran wrap and let double again, about 2 hours.
7. Preheat oven to 400°F. Punch the dough down slightly. Bake for about 8 minutes, then brush remaining olive oil on top and garnish with sea salt. Bake for another 8–10 minutes or until golden. Let rest about 5 minutes before slicing.

PUMPKIN SPICE BISCUITS

Oh pumpkin spice biscuits, how much I adore you. You are flakey, layered with my favorite flavors, and taste exactly what I think a crisp fall morning would taste like. Pumpkin spice biscuits, if I had to choose a favorite, I have to say, you're definitely it. But *shh*, don't tell the others.

Yields about 12 biscuits

Ingredients:

- 1½ cups all-purpose flour + more for dusting
- ½ cup whole wheat flour
- 2½ teaspoons baking powder
- 1½ teaspoons pumpkin pie spice
- 3 tablespoons unsalted butter
- 2 tablespoons unsweetened applesauce
- ⅓ cup light cream or low-fat buttermilk
- ¾ cup canned pumpkin puree (NOT pumpkin pie mix)
- 1 tablespoons honey
- 2 tablespoons brown sugar

Nutritional information per biscuit:

Calories: 115.7

Fat: 3.4 grams

Carbohydrates: 20.8 grams

Protein: 3.2 grams

Fiber: 1.6 grams

Directions:

1. Preheat oven to 400°F. Line a baking sheet with parchment paper and lightly grease that with nonstick cooking spray. Set aside.

2. In a large bowl, mix flours, baking powder, pumpkin pie spice, and salt together. Using a pastry knife, cut in butter and applesauce until mixture resembles a course sand. Cover with saran wrap and chill for at least 10 minutes. Once chilled, mix in the cream, canned pumpkin, honey, and brown sugar until just combined.

3. Scoop dough onto a lightly floured surface. Knead it about 3–4 times, adding extra flour because the dough will be a little moist. Once dough has been kneaded, flour a rolling pin. Roll the dough out to about a ½-inch thickness. Fold it over in half and reroll it out to another ½-inch thickness. Fold it over in half again and reroll. Repeat this one more time, this time rolling it out to about a ¾-inch thickness. Using a circular biscuit cutter or cookie cutter, cut out biscuits.

4. Place biscuits about 1-inch apart on the prepared cooking sheet. Bake for about 12–14 minutes. Let cool and then enjoy!

HOW TO MAKE YOUR OWN PUMPKIN PIE SPICE:

Mix 4 tablespoons ground cinnamon, 4 teaspoons ground nutmeg, 4 teaspoons ground ginger, and about 3 teaspoons ground allspice. Store in an airtight container for easy use!

FRESH CORN AND PEPPER CORNBREAD

Prior to starting my blog when I was just a poor student, I thought good cornbread came in a Jiffy box. When I had my first taste of real homemade cornbread speckled with chunks of fresh from the ear corn and spicy jalapeño, well, I think I passed out. Even if you don't have a lot of time or don't feel like baking, make this fresh corn and pepper cornbread. You'll never regret it (like you do that one night in college when you spent the night with that strange guy from linguistics class).

Serves about 12

Ingredients:

- 1 cup unsweetened applesauce
- 4 tablespoons unsalted butter, softened
- 4 eggs, room temperature
- 2 cups fresh corn, cut off the cob
- 1 jalapeño pepper, seeded and chopped
- 1 habanero pepper, seeded and chopped
- 1 cup part-skim shredded cheddar cheese
- 1 cup all-purpose flour
- 1 cup yellow cornmeal
- 4 teaspoons baking powder
- Dash of salt and pepper
- ½ cup chopped cilantro

Nutritional information per serving (1 slice):

Calories: 184.3

Fat: 6.2 grams

Carbohydrates: 25 grams

Protein: 7 grams

Fiber: 3.4 grams

Directions:

1. Preheat oven to 300°F. Grease a baking dish with nonstick cooking spray (we used an 8 x 8-inch pan).
2. In a large bowl, cream the butter and applesauce together. Add eggs, one at a time, until fully combined. Stir in fresh corn, jalapeño, habanero, cheese, flour, baking powder, salt, and cornmeal. Stir to combine.
3. Pour mixture into the prepared pan. Bake for about 1 hour and 5 minutes or until a toothpick inserted comes out clean.
4. Cut into bite-size pieces and garnish with fresh cilantro.

WHOLE WHEAT LEMON YOGURT BREAD

You know what differentiates an amazing quick bread from a "so-so" one? I'll give you one hint, it rhymes with hogurt. The addition of low-fat yogurt keeps each scrumptious slice of this whole wheat lemon bread moist and soft.

Yields 1 loaf

Ingredients:

- 1 egg
- ½ teaspoon salt
- ½ teaspoon baking soda
- ¾ cup sugar
- 1½ cup whole wheat flour
- ⅓ cup canola oil
- 1 cup low-fat plain Greek yogurt
- 2 tablespoons lemon juice
- 2 teaspoons grated lemon peel
- ½ teaspoon vanilla
- ¼ teaspoon baking powder
- ¾ cup powdered sugar
- Cooking spray

Nutritional information per slice:

Calories: 242

Fat: 8.7 grams

Carbohydrates: 46.8 grams

Protein: 5.4 grams

Fiber: 2.4 grams

Directions:

1. Preheat oven to 325°F.
2. Squeeze lemon juice from a fresh lemon. Then grate the peel.
3. Combine flour, sugar, salt, baking powder, and baking soda into a bowl.
4. In another bowl, stir egg, oil, yogurt, 1 tablespoon of lemon juice, and lemon peel. Once mixed, add dry ingredients to wet ingredients. Mix well.
5. Pour mixture into a greased loaf pan.
6. Bake for 45 minutes.
7. While baking, mix together the sugar and remaining lemon juice to create a glaze.
8. When bread is done baking and has COMPLETELY cooled, apply glaze. I do this by grabbing a spoon and weaving the glaze over the bread in zigzags.

LOW-FAT DINER-STYLE BISCUITS

I have many weaknesses when it comes to food. Like bacon, salted chocolate, and goat cheese, to name a few. However, there is one food in particular that I, literally, have absolutely no control over when it's around me. That food? Diner style biscuits. Which is why I only make this recipe when a craving hits. Each biscuit is flakey and buttery, but has far less fat and calories than regular biscuits. Because don't we all have enough to feel guilty about on a daily basis? Must we add "ate fifteen diner biscuits" to that list?

Yields about 12 biscuits

Ingredients:

- 2 cups of all-purpose flour
- 2½ teaspoons baking powder
- Dash of salt
- 5 tablespoons cold butter, cut into slices
- ½ cup light cream
- ¼ cup milk
- 2½ tablespoons sugar

Nutritional information per biscuit:

Calories: 132

Fat: 6.8 grams

Carbohydrates: 22 grams

Protein: 4 grams

Fiber: 1 gram

Directions:

1. Mix together the flour, baking powder, and salt in a medium size mixing bowl. Using a pastry blender, add the butter and cut into the flour mixture until it resembles a coarse meal. It's okay if you have small chunks of butter, that's what you want! Cover and chill for at least 10 minutes.

2. Once chilled, add the light cream and sugar and mix until just combined. Place dough on a lightly floured surface and knead about 4 times. To roll them out, use a rolling pin and roll out to about the size of a 9 x 5 rectangle. Then fold the dough vertically in thirds. You should have a thin, tall rectangle of dough. Roll dough back out to a 9 x 5 rectangle and then fold again crosswise in thirds. Then, roll the dough out to about ¾–1 inch thickness. Using a small circular cookie cutter (or ⅓ measuring cup dusted with flour) cut out biscuits.

3. Preheat oven to 400°F and lightly grease a baking sheet with non-stick cooking spray. Place biscuits about an inch apart on the baking sheet and bake for 10–12 minutes or until they've puffed up and are golden brown. Serve immediately and enjoy!

FLUFFY BISCUIT TIP: Want those amazing buttery layers you see in those to-die-for diner biscuits? Fold the dough. Fold it over and over and over again. When you think you've folded it too much, fold it once more. This will result in sky-high biscuits with a ton of flakey, delicious layers!

RASPBERRY, BLUEBERRY, AND LEMON LOAF (EGG-FREE)

Or as it should be called, "Heavenly Cake from the Gods." This quick bread, which is filled with fresh berries and topped with a sweet blueberry glaze, is more like a cake, but I'm calling it a bread so you can have it for breakfast without the judgment stares. You can thank me in the form of a loaf in the mail.

Yields 1 loaf (serves about 8)

Ingredients:

- 2 cups all-purpose flour
- ¼ cup white sugar
- 1 tablespoon honey
- 2½ teaspoons baking powder
- Dash of salt
- ½ cup low-fat milk
- ½ cup nonfat Greek yogurt
- ¾ cup unsweetened applesauce
- ¼ cup oil
- 1 pint fresh raspberries
- ½ pint fresh blueberries
- Zest from 1 medium lemon
- 2 tablespoons lemon juice
- ¼ cup chopped walnuts

> **Nutritional information per slice:**
>
> Calories: 278
>
> Fat: 10 grams
>
> Carbohydrates: 45 grams
>
> Protein: 7 grams
>
> Fiber: 3.4 grams

Directions:

1. Preheat oven to 350°F. Grease a loaf pan with baking spray.
2. Whisk the flour, sugar, baking powder, and salt together. Set aside.
3. In another bowl, beat the yogurt, applesauce, lemon zest, lemon juice, cream, milk, and honey together. Make a well in the center of the flour mixture and add to combine.
4. Carefully fold in the blueberries and raspberries. Pour the batter into the prepared loaf pan. Sprinkle the top of the loaf with nuts.
5. Bake for about 65-70 minutes or until golden brown and a toothpick inserted in the middle comes out clean.

EGG-FREE BAKING: My favorite egg replacer in baked goods like cookies, cakes, and quick breads is applesauce. It not only works to bind the fats, it makes the end result super moist!

ALLERGIC TO EGGS? CHECK OUT THESE SUBSTITUTES!

1 egg = ¼ cup mashed sweet or regular potatoes

1 egg = ¼ cup unsweetened applesauce

1 egg = 1 banana

1 egg = 1 tablespoon ground flax seed plus
        3 tablespoons hot water

1 egg = ¼ cup pureed prunes or plums

1 egg = ¼ cup pureed SOFT tofu

GLUTEN-FREE BAKED APPLE CIDER BREAD

Gluten-free baking is something that is near and dear to me. One of my best friends has a severe gluten allergy and it broke my heart when she saw my plates and stands filled with freshly baked goods when she came over. Now whenever I can, I experiment with gluten-free goodies. This apple cider bread is a favorite of mine, and hers. Each slice is loaded with fresh chunks of apple and cinnamon. You wouldn't know it was gluten-free unless I told you. And according to her, that's when you know it's a good recipe.

Yields 1 loaf (about 12 slices)

Ingredients:

- 2 cups gluten-free flour
- 1½ teaspoons xanthan gum
- 1 teaspoon baking powder
- 1 teaspoon baking soda
- 2½ teaspoons apple pie or pumpkin pie spice
- 2 tablespoons unsweetened applesauce
- 2 tablespoons butter, softened
- ½ cup brown sugar
- ⅓ cup white sugar
- 2 large eggs, room temperature
- ½ cup apple cider
- 2 cups chopped granny smith apples

Nutritional information per slice:

Calories: 124.2

Fat: 3.3 grams

Carbohydrates: 22.8 grams

Protein: 2.3 grams

Fiber: 1.1 grams

Directions:

1. Preheat oven to 350°F. Grease a standard size loaf pan with nonstick cooking spray.
2. In a large bowl, whisk the flour, xanthan gum, baking powder, baking soda, and spice. Set aside.
3. In another bowl, beat the butter, applesauce, sugars, and eggs. Add the flour mixture to the egg mixture alternating with the flour mixture. Stir in the apples.
4. Pour the batter into the prepared loaf pan and bake for about 55 minutes or until golden brown. Place on a wire cooling rack and let cool.

GF BAKING TIP: Although many gluten-free flours don't require xanthan gum, adding it will result in a bread with more viscosity and volume.

SKINNY
SNACKS

After school snacks were an institution in my house when I was growing up. As soon as we pulled into our driveway and threw our backpacks carelessly onto the family room floor, my brothers and I would make our way into the kitchen, scouring the cabinets, fridge, and pantry for the perfect afternoon snack. Candy bars, chips, and queso, a few sleeves of nutter butters meant that for today school was over and I could finally relax.

Even though I've been out of school for . . . well, longer than I'd care to admit, I still love having an "after-school" snack. For me, that usually happens after a long day of writing or cooking, or during the mid-afternoon slump when I can't seem to string a sentence together to save my life. Instead of nutter butters or chips though, I enjoy one of these tried and true snack time favorites, like rich pumpkin and butterscotch granola bars or a spicy buffalo chicken quinoa bite. Each of these snacks is filled with healthy ingredients like oats, quinoa, or broccoli and all have less than 300 calories so I can nosh without a side of guilt.

PUMPKIN WHITE CHOCOLATE CHIP BUTTERSCOTCH GRANOLA BARS

Many people say that baking cookies before you show a house to sell it is a good way to entice potential buyers. I want to politely dispute that. If you really want someone to buy your house, make these pumpkin white chocolate chip butterscotch granola bars. The smell is so intoxicating, people will be far too distracted to notice any gaping holes or roofing problems.

Yields about 12 bars

Ingredients:

- 3 cups old fashioned oats
- 1¼ teaspoons pumpkin pie spice
- ¼ cup sugar
- ¼ cup plus 1 tablespoon brown sugar
- ½ cup pumpkin puree
- 3 tablespoons unsalted butter
- 1 tablespoon unsweetened applesauce
- ¼ cup honey
- 1 teaspoon vanilla extract
- ⅔ cup white chocolate chips
- ⅓ cup butterscotch chips

Nutritional information per slice:

Calories: 242

Fat: 9.3 grams

Carbohydrates: 39.8 grams

Protein: 2.9 grams

Fiber: 1 gram

Directions:

1. Preheat oven to 350°F. Spray an 8 x 8-inch baking pan with cooking spray and set aside.
2. In a large mixing bowl, mix the oats and spices together.
3. In another bowl, beat the butter, applesauce, brown sugar, pumpkin puree, honey, and vanilla together. Stir in the butterscotch and white chocolate chips.
4. Press the mixture into the prepared pan. Bake for about 30 minutes or until golden (and very fragrant).
5. Let cool and then cut into bars.

BUFFALO CHICKEN QUINOA BITES

Buffalo wings are one of my biggest weaknesses. I can never have just one. Luckily for me, these buffalo chicken quinoa bites taste just like the wings without all the self-loathing that comes with them. Spicy and filled with healthy fats, proteins, and fiber, these will fill you up and satisfy your wing craving.

Yields about 8 bites

Ingredients:

- 1 cup cooked quinoa
- 1 egg, room temperature
- ¼ cup chopped yellow onion
- 2 cloves garlic, minced
- ¼ cup buffalo sauce
- 1 cup shredded chicken
- ⅓ cup part-skim mozzarella cheese
- 2½ tablespoons blue cheese, crumbled
- ½ cup Panko breadcrumbs
- 2½ tablespoons chopped chives
- Salt and pepper

Nutritional information per bite:

Calories: 132.2

Fat: 4.3 grams

Carbohydrates: 7.68 grams

Protein: 13 grams

Fiber: 2 grams

Directions:

1. Preheat oven to 350°F. Grease a muffin tin with nonstick cooking spray and set aside.
2. In a large bowl, mix the egg, onion, quinoa, garlic, buffalo sauce, chicken, mozzarella cheese, blue cheese, Panko breadcrumbs, chives, and salt and pepper.
3. Press the mixture into the prepared muffin tin. Fill about ¾ the way full.
4. Bake for about 25 minutes or until set. Serve warm.

VEGAN QUESO BLANCO DIP

There's a Mexican place a few blocks from where I used to work in Washington DC that makes the best queso dip. It's so good, you practically want to spoon-feed it to yourself between sips of margarita. I wanted to recreate it at home, but with my own healthier twist, which is where this vegan queso blanco dip came from. I spent months trying to find the perfectly cheesy, creamy, and slightly spicy dip and finally, it hit me. You'll definitely want to eat this with a spoon, trust me!

Serves about 6

Ingredients:

- ¼ cup diced onions
- 1 cup Daiya mozzarella cheese style shreds
- ½ cup Daiya cheddar style shreds
- ⅔ cup chipotle chunky salsa
- Fresh tomato, chopped*
- Salt and pepper
- Fresh cilantro, chopped

Nutritional information per serving:

Calories: 100

Fat: 6 grams

Carbohydrates: 9.5 grams

Protein: 1.5 grams

Fiber: >1 gram

Directions:

1. In a saucepan over medium heat, add mozzarella shreds, cheddar shreds, chunky salsa, onion, salt, and pepper. Heat for about 4 minutes or until melted.
2. Stir in fresh cilantro and chopped tomatoes and serve with chips.

*Chopped tomato is totally optional. It adds a nice added chunkiness to the queso.

BAKED MOZZARELLA SNACK BITES

Hi mozzarella sticks. Yes, it's me Claire. I know you've tried calling and left a few voicemails. I've been meaning to call you back. But, you see, there's no easy way to say this. I'm moving on. You see, there's another cheesy snack in my life and well, it treats me better than you did. It doesn't make me feel bad about myself or make my pants inexplicably tighter. It makes me feel good, and happy. So, I'm sorry to say, we're through. I'm just too in love with my new baked mozzarella snack bites.

Serves about 4

Ingredients:

- 8 ounces fresh mini mozzarella balls (found near the regular logs of fresh mozzarella)
- ¼ all-purpose flour
- ¼ cup whole wheat flour
- 1 egg, beaten
- 1½ cups Panko breadcrumbs
- 2 tablespoons fresh Parmesan cheese
- 1 tablespoon Italian seasoning

Nutritional information per serving:

Calories: 303

Fat: 14 grams

Carbohydrates: 28.25 grams

Protein: 16.25 grams

Fiber: 0 grams

Directions:

1. Place the mini mozzarella balls onto a parchment paper lined baking sheet and freeze for about 2 hours.
2. Mix the breadcrumbs, cheese, and Italian seasoning together.
3. Once frozen, roll the balls into flour. Then roll in the egg and dredge in the breadcrumbs.
4. Place the balls on another parchment paper lined baking sheet. Preheat oven to 450°F.
5. Bake for about 8–10 minutes or until breadcrumbs are golden brown. Serve immediately with marinara.

CREAMY WHITE BEAN AND BROCCOLI DIP

This dip was made for skinny Super Bowl eating. It's creamy, thick, and full of amazing flavors like cilantro, lime, toasted pine nuts, and pepper. It's a symphony in your mouth. And the best part ever? It has only 5 grams of fat per ¼ cup serving! Which trust me, you won't have any trouble consuming.

Yields about 2½ cups (serves about 10)

Ingredients:

- 1 can (15 ounces) white cannelloni beans, drained
- 1 small head of broccoli, cut into florets
- 2 cloves garlic
- ¾ cup chopped carrots
- 2 tablespoons olive oil
- 2 ounces low-fat cream cheese
- Salt and pepper
- About ¼ cup chopped cilantro
- Juice from one lime
- About 2 tablespoons pine nuts
- About 2 tablespoons water*

Nutritional information
per ¼ cup:

Calories: 114

Fat: 5 grams

Carbohydrates: 11.7 grams

Protein: 4.9 grams

Fiber: 2.75 grams

*Add water if mixture is too thick.

Directions:

1. Preheat oven to 425°F. Grease a baking dish liberally with nonstick cooking spray. Add broccoli, carrots, and garlic to the pan. Liberally season with salt and pepper. Roast for about 10–12 minutes or until nicely browned. Remove from pan and place into a food processor. Add white beans, cream cheese, olive oil, cilantro, lime juice, and salt and pepper. Pulse on low until mixture is thick and smooth. Add water if too thick.

2. In a skillet over medium heat, toast pine nuts for about 3 minutes, stirring constantly. Garnish the dip with pine nuts and additional cilantro and enjoy!

GUILT-FREE APPETIZERS

Appetizers are more than just little puffs of pastry or small and crunchy canapés. Appetizers set the mood, the ambiance, and the tone of your entire meal. Creating appetizers is one of the most challenging parts of my job. Unlike a pizza, a burger, or a salad, where you have an entire canvas to work with, with an appetizer, you have a small puzzle piece, a corner of that blank canvas to turn into a masterpiece. You have just once chance and one bite to really wow your guests. That's a lot of pressure for a little canapé, don't you think?

But if there's one thing I've learned from two years of recipe development (and over twenty-seven years as an avid eater), it's best not to overthink it. When you overthink, you second-guess, when you second-guess, the whole thing goes to sh**, pardon my French. Which is why these appetizers are some of my all-time favorites. Every bite and every small inch of that canvas is exploding with flavor but the package itself is understated while still being elegant. The taste is simple, but stunning.

I know not every party you'll throw will be fancy and sometimes your guests will be under the age of five, so I've created a recipe for any party or gathering you can think of. Crispy vegetarian eggrolls for a play date with your kid's friends, stunning strawberry and balsamic toasts for that fancy party with your husband's boss, and bite-size cantaloupe and arugula bites for book club with the girls. Each recipe is easy yet sophisticated and will instantly turn any get-together into something to remember.

CRISPY VEGETARIAN EGGROLLS

Eggrolls, who can resist them? Crispy, flakey, deep-fried rolls filled with a delicious assortment of meats, vegetables, and slaw. Since I'm perpetually on a diet, I decided to turn my favorite "once in a while indulgence" into a "can eat everyday" snack with this recipe! The rolls are baked, not fried, and are filled with a light vegetarian filling. You'll never want takeout again.

Yields about 20 egg rolls

Ingredients:

- 1 package (8 ounces) Gimme Lean Ground Beef Style (vegetarian protein)
- 1 small yellow onion, chopped
- 3 cloves garlic, diced
- ½ package (7 ounces) broccoli slaw
- 1½ tablespoons soy sauce
- 20 eggroll wrappers
- About 2 egg whites
- 1–2 tablespoons water
- Sriracha for glaze

Nutritional information per roll:

Calories: 120

Fat: 0 grams

Carbohydrates: 22.1 grams

Protein: 6.65 grams

Fiber: 1.5 grams

Directions:

1. Spray a skillet with nonstick cooking spray. Add onions and cook until translucent, about 4 minutes. Add in garlic and beef style. Using a spatula, break the beef up. Heat for about 5 minutes or until fully cooked.
2. Mix in the soy sauce, garlic powder, and salt and pepper. Stir in broccoli slaw.
3. Preheat oven to 375°F.
4. To make the eggrolls, position the wrappers so they are shaped like a diamond. Place about 1 tablespoon of beef mixture into the center of the wrapper. Fold the bottom part of the wrapper up, over the filling. Then fold the two sides over the filling and crease to close.
5. Mix the egg white and water together. Brush the tops of the rolls with egg wash.
6. Bake for about 15 minutes or until golden brown. Serve with a drizzle of Sriracha for some extra heat.

STRAWBERRY, GOAT CHEESE & BALSAMIC CROSTINIS

As a recipe developer, I rarely make the same things twice. I'm always crafting new, exciting, innovative recipes, so if one succeeds, I move onto something different. Well, that was until I made these strawberries, goat cheese, and honey balsamic crostinis. Since their inception a year ago, I've made them ten times. Some recipes are just too good to mess with.

Serves about 4 (2 crostinis each)

Ingredients:

- 8 slices crusty French bread
- 4 tablespoons soft goat cheese
- ½ cup strawberries, smashed
- 2 tablespoons balsamic vinegar
- ¼ cup honey
- Dash of salt

Nutritional information
per canapè:

Calories: 177

Fat: 7 grams

Carbohydrates: 21 grams

Protein: 7 grams

Fiber: 1 gram

Directions:

1. Preheat oven to 400°F. Place the bread on a baking dish and bake for about 4–5 minutes or until golden brown.
2. Top each slice of bread with about 1½ teaspoons of goat cheese. Top the cream cheese with about 1 tablespoon of smashed strawberries.
3. Heat the honey in a microwave and whisk in the balsamic vinegar. Drizzle over the crostinis.

PROSCIUTTO WRAPPED SKEWERS WITH CANTALOUPE AND ARUGULA

For me, entertaining should be three things. Fun, elegant, and easy. These cantaloupe wrapped skewers with prosciutto and arugula encompass all three. They take less than five minutes to make but look like they took thirty.

Yields about 10

Ingredients:

- 1¼ cups sliced cantaloupe cubes (about 1-inch)
- 4 ounces fresh mozzarella
- 10 thin sliced pieces of prosciutto (about ¼ pound)
- ½ cup fresh arugula
- Salt and pepper
- 6 medium skewers

Nutritional information per bite:

Calories: 71.1

Fat: 4.5 grams

Carbohydrates: 2 grams

Protein: 6.2 grams

Fiber: 2.3 grams

Directions:

1. Cut the mozzarella into 1-inch pieces. Place a piece on top of the cantaloupe, add a few sprigs of arugula, and then wrap into prosciutto. Sprinkle with salt and pepper.
2. Serve immediately.

PROSCUITTO TIP: This recipe works best with very thinly sliced prosciutto. Ask your butcher to slice it paper-thin for easy wrapping.

BLT STUFFED MUSHROOM CAPS

One of my uncle George's favorite quotes is this: "You know what goes really well with bacon? MORE BACON!" Which is a sentiment I very much agree with. These BLT stuffed mushroom caps are topped with bits of deliciously crispy bacon, giving each bite a salty little crunch.

Yields about 12 mushrooms

Ingredients:

- 12 large cremini or baby bella mushrooms, stems discarded
- 2 tablespoons extra virgin olive oil
- 1½ tablespoons bread crumbs
- 3 ounces fresh goat cheese, formed into 12 pieces
- 1 plum tomato, freshly diced
- About ¾–1 cup chopped lettuce
- 1 tablespoon Greek yogurt
- 1 tablespoon low-fat mayo
- 2–3 pieces turkey bacon, cooked and crumbled
- Salt and pepper to taste

Nutritional information per bite:

Calories: 77

Fat: 5.5 grams

Carbohydrates: 3.75 grams

Protein: 3.1 grams

Fiber: >1 gram

Directions:

1. Preheat oven to 400°F. Grease a baking sheet with nonstick cooking spray and set aside.
2. Toss the mushrooms with olive oil. Season with salt and pepper. Place, cavity side up, on the baking sheet. Bake for about 30 minutes, or until soft.
3. Once mushrooms have cooled slightly, carefully press the goat cheese into the bottom of each mushroom cap. Sprinkle with breadcrumbs, salt, and pepper.
4. Mix the lettuce, tomatoes, and Greek yogurt and mayo together. Add about one teaspoon over the top of the breadcrumbs. Top the lettuce/tomato mixture with bacon bits.
5. Garnish with salt and pepper.

CRAB CAKE SLIDERS WITH AVOCADO SPREAD

You know what I love most about football games and lazy Sundays? The snacks I get to enjoy while the game is on. I could care less about the teams or the scores, I just love the food. (Surprise, surprise.) These crab cake sliders turn my favorite wedding food into the perfect game day snack with a bit of avocado spread and two toasted slider buns. They're easy to make ahead too for tailgates!

Yields about 8-10 sliders

Ingredients:

For the crab cakes:

- 1 pounds fresh lump crabmeat
- ⅓ cup wheat crackers, crumbled into fine crumbs
- 2 tablespoons egg whites
- 2-3 tablespoons low-fat mayo
- 1 teaspoon spicy Dijon mustard
- About 1 teaspoon Old Bay seasoning
- ¼ teaspoon ground pepper
- 12 slider buns, slightly toasted

**Nutritional information
per slider:**

Calories: 295.9

Fat: 5.6 grams

Carbohydrates: 39.7 grams

Protein: 19.3 grams

Fiber: 0.2 grams

For the spread:

- 1 medium ripe avocado, seeded and pitted
- Juice from ½ lime
- 2 tablespoons chopped green onion
- Liberal dashes of salt and pepper

Directions:

1. Mix ½ crumbles with mayonnaise, mustard, Old Bay seasoning, salt, pepper, and egg whites.
2. Gently fold in the crab and mix until crab is covered in mayonnaise-cracker mixture. Carefully fold into 12 mini crab cakes and place into a greased pan. Chill for at least one hour.
3. Once crab has been chilled, carefully remove from the greased pan. Cover each cake in remaining cracker crumbs to form a crust.
4. Heat olive oil in a medium pan. Place crab cakes oil and fry on both sides until browned, about 4-6 minutes.
5. While crab cakes are frying, make the spread by mashing the avocado, lime juice, green onion, and salt and pepper.

CRAB CAKE TIP: Since these sliders are small, you can buy claw meat, which is generally less expensive than jumbo lump. Regardless of the kind you buy, be sure your crabmeat is fresh. It should have a seawater smell and be slightly mushy.

SLIMMING SOUPS

F all is my favorite time of year. To me, fall has always been so forgiving. I've never been very comfortable with my body, so summer was never an easy season for me. I hated being exposed, having to show off my imperfections. Which is why I loved fall. I could hide in a sweatshirt and jeans and seemingly fit in with the girls who looked far better than me. I could truly play with my cousins or my friends without fear that they were judging my thunder thighs or my slightly chubby stomach. Like the trees that shed their leaves every fall, I'm able to shed my insecurities, and start a whole new season with a fresh new perspective.

Growing up in the Midwest, we were blessed with a true autumn, not like the one I get here in Northern Virginia. The leaves would turn vibrant shades of red, orange, and yellow and would fall in beautiful succession, almost to the tune of some song heard only by them. Right around September, like clockwork, the temperatures would fall and the smells from my mom's kitchen would turn from grilled meat to cozy, comforting soups and stews. After a long day of raking lea-ves, we'd come in to the incredible smells of homemade chicken noodle simmering on the stove or spicy and chunky chili slow cooking in the Crock-Pot. Soup, to me, has magical powers. It can instantly warm you up, make you feel comforted and new. It can turn you from sad to content with just a few warm and flavorful spoonfuls. Soup season is one I count down for and welcome with open arms.

But soup isn't something that's just for chillier months, which is why I've made some feel-good soups that can be enjoyed even in the hot summer months. Like tart strawberry gazpacho or fresh corn and sweet pepper chowder. But for those cold autumn and winter nights, I've created some true "feel-good" soups and stews like chunky pumpkin chili and creamy jalapeño popper. Plus some easy Crock-Pot ideas for when you don't have the time to simmer or stir. No matter the season or the weather, soup's always on my menu!

CHUNKY PUMPKIN TURKEY CHILI

Many people think I'm a little weird for saying things like "I love this chili so much I want to date it." That is until they take one bite. This chunky pumpkin chili is so good, you'll want to take it out to dinner. Or marry it. Or shower it with flowers and gifts. Because that's what a chili of this awesomeness deserves.

Serves about 10

Ingredients:

- 3 small shallots, chopped
- 4 cloves garlic, sliced
- ½ cup chopped mushrooms
- 1 tablespoon olive oil
- 2¾ cups vegetable broth
- ¼ cup dry red wine
- 30 ounces (2 cans) black beans, drained and rinsed
- 14 ounces ground turkey (98 percent lean)
- 1 can (15 ounces) pumpkin
- 1 can (14½ ounces) diced tomatoes, not drained
- 1 tablespoon chili powder
- 2 tablespoons Italian seasoning
- Liberal dashes of salt and pepper

Nutritional information per ½ cup serving:

Calories: 177.7

Fat: 3 grams

Carbohydrates: 29.2 grams

Protein: 3.5 grams

Fiber: 11.7 grams

Directions:

1. Heat oil in a large pan. Add shallots, garlic, and mushrooms. Cook until fragrant and soft, about 4 minutes. Remove from heat and pour into the basin of a Crock-Pot.

2. Add the turkey chili and break up with a spatula. Cook for about 4–5 minutes or until browned. Pour in broth, wine, black beans, diced tomatoes, and pumpkin. Stir to mix up the ingredients. Sprinkle in salt, pepper, chili powder, and Italian seasoning.

3. Set the Crock-Pot to low and cook for 6–8 hours. Serve with cornbread or your favorite bread and enjoy!

ROAST DUCK SOUP

I don't typically use or order duck because it's a fattier meat and it has a REALLY bold flavor. Plus, it's often served with that weird fruit jelly stuff and that freaks me out. However, after a bit of experimenting I found a recipe that highlights the bold flavor while giving me the warm and fuzzies. This soup was like eating comfort and childhood in a big bowl. The broth was perfectly flavored with roasted vegetables and a dash of low-sodium soy sauce and the duck was melt in your mouth tender. Paired with some slightly crunchy bok choy stems and wilted leaves and you have an amazing and healthy bowl of goodness.

Serves about 4

Ingredients:

- 2 duck breasts
- 1 tablespoon extra virgin olive oil
- 2 carrots, chopped
- ½ medium onion, chopped
- 4 cloves of garlic, chopped
- 1 quart reduced sodium chicken broth
- 8 ounces rice noodles
- 2 tablespoons low-sodium soy sauce
- Salt and pepper to taste
- 2 cups chopped bok choy

> ### Nutritional information
> ### per ¾ cup serving:
> Calories: 310
> Fat: 9 grams
> Carbohydrates: 32 grams
> Protein: 22 grams
> Fiber: 3 grams

Directions:

1. Place the rice noodles in a bowl of hot water until just softened, about 15 minutes.
2. Preheat oven to 375°F. Score the sides of the duck's skin with a knife. Place duck in a glass baking dish coated with olive oil. Add carrots, onion, and garlic. Roast for about 40-50 minutes, or until duck is brown and slightly pink on the inside. Remove from pan and cut off fat and skin. Cut the duck into bite size pieces and set aside.
3. While duck roasts, heat broth and soy sauce. Place roasted vegetables and duck into the broth and reduce heat to low. Simmer duck and vegetables for about 10 more minutes. Add in noodles and chopped bok choy. Heat until bok choy is just softened. Season with a dash of salt and pepper and enjoy!

LOWER-SODIUM FRENCH ONION SOUP

When I was in Paris, I ordered a bowl of onion soup at nearly every bistro I went to. I told my mom I was doing "onion soup research" for my articles, but in all reality, I just couldn't get enough of it. I knew I wanted to make a recipe for this book but one with a smidge less sodium and all of the delicious flavor you'd expect in a truly authentic bowl of French onion soup. After testing four different recipes, this one won by a landslide. It's what I make when I'm so heartsick for Paris I can barely stand it.

Yields about 8 servings

Ingredients:

- 3 tablespoons unsalted butter
- 6 large onions, sliced
- 44 ounces low-sodium, fat-free beef broth
- 1 cup dark beer
- 1 cup water
- 1 bay leaf
- 8 small slices French bread, cut in half
- 4 slices Muenster cheese, cut in half
- Salt and pepper to taste

> **Nutritional information per serving (about ⅔ cup soup and bread):**
>
> Calories: 228
>
> Fat: 10.25 grams
>
> Carbohydrates: 28 grams
>
> Protein: 9.75 grams
>
> Fiber: 2.3 grams

Directions:

1. Melt butter in a large Dutch oven over medium heat. Add onions and reduce heat to low. Cover the onions and let simmer for 30 minutes or until completely caramelized. Pour in beer, a dash of salt, and bay leaf.
2. Bring the mixture to a boil and then reduce to a simmer.
3. Add beef broth and cover mixture again and let simmer for another 20 minutes or until very fragrant.
4. Remove from heat and pour into 8 bowls or single serve Le Creuset cocottes. Top each ramekin with a slice of bread and cheese.
5. Preheat the broiler. Place the ramekins on a cake pan and broil for about 2-4 minutes or until cheese is melted.

FRENCH ONION SOUP TIP: The slower you cook the onions, the more flavor they will release. Let them cook until they are perfectly caramelized and almost tender to the touch. This will give your broth that truly authentic onion flavor.

BRUSSELS SPROUT SAUSAGE SOUP

My favorite part of this soup is how VEGGIETASTIC it is. It's literally filled to the brim with fiber rich, good for you veggies. I can't even stand how good this soup is for your bodies, friends. This soup will set you back to your pre-Thanksgiving, pre-baby, pre-that pint of Ben and Jerry's ice cream dinner weight and will probably cure any ailment you have plaguing you.

Serves about 6 (⅔ cup servings)

Ingredients:

- 2 cups of Brussels sprouts, quartered
- 1 cup sliced carrots
- 1 cup sliced celery
- 1 cup sliced chickens sausage
- ½ cup sliced rotisserie chicken
- 1 medium onion, chopped
- 2 cloves garlic, minced
- 4½ cups low-sodium chicken broth
- 1 bay leaf
- 2 tablespoons crushed red pepper
- Salt and pepper to taste

Nutritional information per serving:

Calories: 178.5

Fat: 8.3 grams

Carbohydrates: 9 grams

Protein: 18.3 grams

Fiber: 8.1 grams

Directions:

1. Place the vegetables, chicken and chicken sausage, and bay leaf into the basin of a Crock-Pot. Pour broth over the mixture and add crushed red pepper, salt and pepper.
2. Set Crock-Pot on medium and cook for 3½ hours, stirring every hour. Reduce heat to low and cook an additional hour or until all vegetables are soft. Serve immediately with crusty bread or dinner rolls!

CORN AND SWEET PEPPER CHOWDER

My friends and my husband think I'm crazy when I suggest we have soup for dinner. In August. When it's 154°F outside. And you know what, I think they're probably right. But if God didn't want us to have soup in summer, why would he invent corn chowder? If you're like my friends and think hot soup in hot weather is nuts, this chowder is just as delicious served chilled. The sweet peppers and corn give it a natural sweetness that is contrasted wonderfully with the spicy jalapeños.

Serves about 6

Ingredients:

- 8 ears corn
- 3 jalapeños, seeded and chopped
- 8–10 sweet peppers, chopped
- 1 medium yellow onion, diced
- 5 cups low-sodium chicken broth
- 2 tablespoons extra virgin olive oil
- ½ cup loosely packed cilantro
- 1 teaspoon Mexican Perfect Pinch seasoning
- Salt and pepper to taste

Nutritional information
per serving:

Calories: 250

Fat: 6.5 grams

Carbohydrates: 33.8 grams

Protein: 8.2 grams

Fiber: 3.2 grams

Directions:

1. Remove the corn from the cob. To do this, simply hold the corn up vertically and carefully drag a knife down (from top to the bottom) cutting the kernels from the ear. Set aside.
2. In a large pot (I use a Dutch oven), heat olive oil over medium-high heat. Add onions, sweet peppers and jalapeños. Heat until onion is translucent, about 5 minutes.
3. Add the corn to the onions and heat about 5 minutes, or until corn starts to soften. Add in 2½ cups broth, ¼ cup chopped cilantro, Mexican seasoning, and salt and pepper.
4. Bring mixture to a boil and then reduce to a simmer. Let simmer for about 15 minutes.
5. Remove from heat. In batches, blend the soup in a high-powdered blender until creamy. Add additional salt and pepper to taste.
6. Serve with additional sliced peppers and cilantro.

TIME SAVING TIP: Don't have time to shuck corn or access to fresh sweet corn? Use cans of sweet corn instead.

STUFFED JALAPEÑO & CHEESE SOUP

This creamy soup with a zesty, spicy jalapeño kick is the answer to any jalapeño popper lover's dreams. Every bowl tastes just like the crispy fried jalapeño poppers you order at popular restaurants, only in a lighter, cheesier, and even creamier version. Topped with crispy French bread, this soup is my version of heaven.

Yields about 4 cups (about 4 servings each)

Ingredients:

- 1 tablespoon extra virgin olive oil
- 4 ounces (½ block) fat-free cream cheese
- ½ cup light cream
- ¼ cup 2 percent milk
- 1¾ cups low-sodium vegetable broth
- 5 jalapeños, seeded and chopped
- 2 small red sweet peppers, chopped
- 1 cup part-skim mozzarella cheese
- ½ cup pepperjack cheese
- 1 tablespoon crushed red pepper
- Salt and pepper to taste
- Crispy French bread for garnish

Nutritional information per serving:

Calories: 256.5

Fat: 17.5 grams

Carbohydrates: 9.25 grams

Protein: 16 grams

Fiber: 4 grams

Directions:

1. Preheat oven to 400°F. Cut two of the jalapeños in half lengthwise and place on a baking sheet. Roast for about 10 minutes on each side or until peppers are softened. Chop and set aside.

2. Heat the olive oil in a large dutch oven over medium heat. Add 3 jalapeños, sweet peppers and crushed red pepper. Cook until softened, about 3 minutes. Add the cream cheese and heat for about 2–3 minutes or until melted.

3. Whisk together the milk and the light cream. Pour over the peppers. Add in vegetable broth and whisk to combine. Stir in the salt, pepper, and crushed red pepper.

4. Reduce heat to low and let soup simmer for about 5–8 minutes or until combined. Add salt and pepper to taste.

5. Remove the soup from the heat and stir in the cheeses and 2 reserved chopped jalapeños. Pour into bowls and garnish with chopped French bread.

BEST VEGAN CHILI YOU'LL EVER EAT

We all have that friend. The one that looks effortlessly gorgeous every time you hang out. The one whose outfit always seems to match just perfectly and has the cutest accessories. The one who always knows the right thing to say and always has the coolest events to go to on weekends. The one who your boyfriend/husband/fiancé secretly has a crush on but will never admit to. Well, this vegan chili is that friend. No matter how many times you make it, it comes out perfect every single time. It really is the best vegan chili you'll ever eat.

Serves 4-6

Ingredients:

- 1 tablespoon extra virgin olive oil
- 14 ounces Gimme Lean Ground Beef Style
- ½ medium yellow bell pepper, chopped
- ½ medium orange bell pepper, chopped
- 1 medium yellow onion, chopped
- 4 cloves garlic, diced
- ¼ cup low-sodium vegetable broth
- 2 cans (15 ounces each) fire roasted diced tomatoes
- 1 can (14.5 ounces) black beans, rinsed
- 1 tablespoon chili powder
- 1 tablespoon ground cumin
- 2 tablespoons chopped thyme
- 1 bunch fresh cilantro, chopped
- Salt and pepper to taste

Nutritional information
per serving:

Calories: 274.5

Fat: 3.6 grams

Carbohydrates: 46.6 grams

Protein: 17.2 grams

Fiber: 13.2 grams

Directions:

1. In a large Dutch oven, heat the olive oil over medium-high heat. Add the onions, garlic, peppers and Gimme Lean Ground Beef Style soy protein. Cook until onions are translucent, about 4 minutes. Pour in the vegetable broth, fire roasted tomatoes, black beans, chili powder, tarragon, and some chopped cilantro.
2. Stir in salt and pepper. Heat the mixture on low and let simmer, covered, for about 15-20 minutes. Serve with fresh cilantro.

TIME SAVING TIP: If you're tight on time, throw all of these ingredients into the basin of your slow cooker and set to low. Let the chili cook, with a few stirs, for about 6-8 hours. You'll have chunky stew without any stress!

SWEET STRAWBERRY & PEPPER GAZPACHO

You know what I love most about strawberries? How elegant they are. They turn any dish into something extraordinary. This beautiful strawberry and pepper gazpacho is prime example of this. The addition of the plump, sweet strawberries gives this chilled soup a sophisticated make-over and a delightful sweetness, making it a dream for hot summer days.

Serves about 2-3

Ingredients:

- 10 large strawberries, hulled and sliced
- 1 large tomato, diced
- 1 large yellow heirloom tomato, diced
- 5 sweet bell peppers, chopped
- Juice from ½ lemon
- ⅓ cup sundried tomatoes
- About 3 tablespoons dry white wine
- Salt and pepper to taste
- Cilantro for garnish
- 1 large strawberry, sliced for garnish

> **Nutritional information per serving:**
>
> Calories: 121.5
>
> Fat: >1 gram
>
> Carbohydrates: 19 grams
>
> Protein: >1 gram
>
> Fiber: 0 grams

Directions:

1. Place all of the ingredients in a high-powdered blender. Pulse on low until pureed and smooth. Add salt and pepper to taste.
2. Serve each bowl with fresh cilantro and sliced strawberries.

BUTTERNUT SQUASH AND APPLE SOUP

Autumn and winter are my favorite seasons. I love curling up in a soft cashmere sweater next to a roaring fire and a pot of homemade soup simmering on the stove. I love being bundled up, watching leaves or snowflakes fall outside and know that I'm warm and comfy inside. This soup evokes those same warm, cozy, and comforting feelings. Made with buttery squash and crisp apples, each spoonful feels as smooth and soft as your favorite sweater.

Serves about 4–6

Ingredients:

- 1 medium yellow onion, diced
- 2 tablespoons unsalted butter, divided
- 1 medium butternut squash
- 1 red apple, diced
- 3½ cups low-sodium chicken broth
- ½ cup apple cider
- Salt and pepper to taste
- Fresh Italian herbs for garnish

Nutritional information per serving:

Calories: 176.25

Fat: 6 grams

Carbohydrates: 30.25 grams

Protein: 3.5 grams

Fiber: >1 gram

Directions:

1. Prepare the butternut squash by preheating the oven to 400°F. With a sharp knife, cut the squash in half lengthwise. Place the squash halves flesh side up on a large baking sheet. Remove the seeds with a spoon and discard.

2. Melt one tablespoon of butter. Brush the butternut squash halves with butter. Sprinkle with salt and pepper. Roast for about 25 minutes or until fork-tender.

3. Let cool slightly then peel and chop.

4. Meanwhile, heat the second tablespoon of butter in a large saucepan. Add the onion and apple and cook until soft and translucent, about 4 minutes. Pour in the low-sodium chicken broth, apple cider, chopped Italian seasoning, and salt and pepper. Cook for about 6–8 minutes.

5. Add the squash to a large, powerful blender. Pour in the cooked soup and puree on low until creamy. Garnish with salt and pepper to taste and serve with fresh herbs.

SUPER CHUNKY LENTIL STEW

If you couldn't tell from my previous recipes, I'm sort of a fan of "chunky" soups and stews. If I'm going to make stew my main meal for the night, it needs to be hearty; something you almost need a fork to eat it with. This super chunky lentil soup is so thick, you'll practically need a wooden spoon to eat it. Lucky for you, hearty doesn't mean bulky or heavy. The lentils give each bowl a punch of fiber and protein without extra fat or calories.

Serves about 4

Ingredients:

- 1 cup dried lentils, red or brown
- 2 cups chicken broth
- 2 cups water
- 2½ tablespoons dry white wine
- ¼ cup chopped onion
- ½ cup chopped celery
- 1½ tablespoons parsley or oregano
- 1 clove garlic
- Salt and pepper
- 1 can (14.5 ounces) diced tomatoes
- Avocado, diced for garnish

Nutritional information per serving:

Calories: 135

Fat: >1 gram

Carbohydrates: 26.5 grams

Protein: 9.25 grams

Fiber: 7.2 grams

Directions:

1. Add the lentils, broth, water, white wine, onion, celery, spices, and garlic to a slow cooker. Stir to mix up.
2. Set to low and cook for 8–10 hours.
3. Check lentils. If they are still crunchy, cook another 3–4 hours. Add tomatoes and cook on high for about one more hour.
4. Serve with fresh herbs and avocado.

WHY I'M GAGA FOR LENTILS:

1. Lentils, which are a type of legume, are naturally low in calories but high in fiber.
2. Lentils help to reduce blood cholesterol due to their high level of fiber. This will help reduce your risk for heart disease!
3. One cup of cooked lentils only has 230 calories with 26 percent of those calories coming from protein.

SKINNY SIPS & COCKTAILS

I've never been much of a "cocktail" girl. When I was in the working world and my coworkers and I would go out for happy hour, I never ordered the cocktail of the day or the cosmopolitans some of my friends would drink. For me, it was always simple: white wine (Chardonnay, to be exact) or a Blue Moon. In the heydays of my youth, I drank a lot of hard liquor so as I've grown up, I've kind of steered clear of it. Well, that was until I started my job with SheKnows.com.

The first few months into my role as a "recipe developer" for SK, I was given a huge assignment. My fabulous editor Joanie called me and told me to create twelve unique cocktails for the recipe portion of the site. I was ecstatic. It was a ton of responsibility and my first real assignment for the website. As soon as the excitement wore off, I realized something; I had no idea how to make a trendy cocktail. Happiness turned to sheer panic as I rushed to my computer, googling "how to make a cosmopolitan" or "the perfect cocktails for parties." I binge-bought boxes of martini glasses, shakers and fun swirly straws, crates of mason jars in all sizes, and fun napkins to make the glasses pop. The first few weeks were rough and there were quite a few fails but I eventually figured it out. After creating twelve cocktails, I found that I really enjoyed mixing drinks and creating fun libations with different flavors.

Now, I make cocktails almost weekly for work. From slimming martinis to decadent boozy milkshakes, making new and innovative drinks for friends and family has become a small passion of mine. In this section you'll find some of my favorite drinks like my infamous banana pie boozy milkshake or my smashed strawberry Bellini. You'll also find my favorite non-alcoholic blackberry lemonade, which is the most refreshing summer drink. Even if you're not a mixologist, I promise you'll have fun making one of these for your family and friends.

BANANA CREAM PIE BOOZY MILKSHAKE

Sometimes a girl just needs a milkshake, am I right? And the only thing better than a thick and creamy milkshake is one that's filled with vodka. I've sort of become the "go-to expert" in the field of boozy milkshakes at work and I'm constantly challenging myself with new and delicious recipes. Of all the shakes I've made (and I'm up to maybe thirty), this banana cream pie shake is one of my favorites. Every sip tastes like my favorite summertime pie, with the much-needed addition of vodka.

Yields 2½ servings (about ¾ cup each)

Ingredients:

- 2 large bananas, frozen and peeled
- ¾ cup nonfat vanilla Chobani
- ¼ cup fat-free vanilla ice cream
- ¼ cup graham crackers, broken into pieces (about ½ sheet)
- 3 tablespoons–¼ cup whipped cream flavored vodka
- 1 tablespoon light cream
- ¼ cup low-fat whipped cream for garnish
- Graham cracker crumbs for garnish

> **Nutritional information per serving:**
> Calories: 300
> Fat: 4.8 grams
> Carbohydrates: 42.5 grams
> Protein: 6.8 grams
> Fiber: >2 grams

Directions:

1. Place the bananas, Greek yogurt, ice cream, vodka, and milk in a blender. Blend until smooth. Add graham crackers and whipped cream and pulse a few times to combine. Add additional vodka for taste (or extra booziness).
2. Pour into mason jars or milkshake glasses and garnish with additional whipped cream and graham cracker crumbs.

BLACKBERRY LEMONADE

I'm spent every summer growing up on Put-In-Bay, which is an island off the coast of Lake Erie in Ohio. Every year my cousins, my brothers, and I would have a lemonade stand in front of the cottage. We'd make giant tubs of tart lemonade and sell it for 15-25 cents a cup. Then, when it was all over and we counted our loot, my dad would take us downtown to the Candy Bar to stock up on Big League Chew and sticky, gooey liquid candy. It is one my most cherished memories. The fresh blackberry lemonade I make now is more sophisticated but every sip reminds me of those summers with my family. And I can't help but smile.

This tart, slightly sweet, and easy to make blackberry lemonade is a perfect picnic drink for warm summer days and nights. Add some vodka or gin for a fun adult only update!

Serves about 4

Ingredients:

- ½ cup white sugar
- ¼ cup honey
- 1 cup water
- 1 cup fresh pressed lemon juice
- 1½ cups fresh blackberries
- 2-3 cups chilled water
- Lemon wedges for garnish

> **Nutritional information per cup:**
>
> Calories: 152
>
> Fat: 0 grams
>
> Carbohydrates: 38 grams
>
> Protein: 0 grams
>
> Fiber: 2 grams

Directions:

1. Bring one cup of water, sugar, and honey to a boil, stirring well for at least three minutes to make a simple syrup. Remove from heat and stir in lemon juice.
2. In a blender, mix one cup of the lemon mixture with blackberries and pulse until fully blended. Strain using a mesh strainer to get rid of seeds. Stir mixture with cold water. Garnish with lemon wedges.

FRESH BERRY MOJITO

The muddled fresh mint, mixed berry puree, and crisp white rum make this cocktail impossible to resist. A big batch of these beautiful and fruity drinks would be the perfect signature cocktail for any spring or summer wedding, party, or picnic!

Serves about 4

Ingredients:

- 3 cups chopped raspberries
- 3 cups blueberries
- About ¼ tablespoon water
- 8 ounces club soda
- 8 ounces mixed berry flavored water
- 8 ounces white rum
- 4 ounces simple syrup
- About 10 mint leaves
- Fresh berries for garnish

Nutritional information per serving:

Calories: 282

Fat: >1 gram

Carbohydrates: 28.5 grams

Protein: 1.75 grams

Fiber: >1 gram

Directions:

1. In a blender, add strawberries and blueberries. Add in water and blend until smooth and pureed.
2. Fill 4 glasses or jars halfway with ice. In a large pitcher, mix the seltzer water, fizzy water, rum, and simple syrup. Pour the mixture into the 4 glasses or jars. Divide the puree in half and pour into each jar or glass.
3. Muddle the mint leaves just slightly to soften. Try to do this carefully so you don't bruise the leaves. Place the leaves in the glasses and garnish with fresh berries.

BOOZY PUMPKIN CIDER

My cousin Liz is the one who got me hooked on "boozy" cider. One winter at her house, she served me a piping mug of fresh apple cider filled with spiced rum and cinnamon. I was sold after my first body-warming sip. To update this delicious drink for fall, I added my favorite seasonal ingredient, pumpkin! Now, no autumn is complete without a big batch of this thick and spicy cider.

Yields about 2 cups

Ingredients:

- ½ cup pumpkin puree (not pumpkin pie mix)
- 2½ cups apple cider
- ¼–⅓ cup spiced rum
- 1½ teaspoons pumpkin pie spice
- Cinnamon stick

Nutritional information per serving:

Calories: 230

Fat: >1 gram

Carbohydrates: 42.5 grams

Protein: 1 grams

Fiber: 0 grams

Directions:

1. In a large pot, mix together the pumpkin puree, apple cider, pumpkin pie spice, and the cinnamon stick.
2. Bring mixture to a boil then reduce heat to low and simmer for at least 20 minutes. If mixture is too thick, add additional cider or water to thin it out.
3. Strain the mixture through a mesh strainer to remove clumps and cinnamon stick. Add rum and mix. Serve warm.

KID-FRIENDLY TIP: Sub in more apple cider in place of the rum for a great family-friendly fall cider.

CHOCOLATE PEPPERMINT BOOZY MILKSHAKE

Dear Santa, I don't know how you do it. I can't even imagine all the stress you have on your shoulders. I'm stressed with my own job and I'm not even the face of a holiday. I just wanted to show my appreciation for what you do in the form of a boozy milkshake. Now, I'll be honest, I almost drank this tonight while I was leaving out your cookies. The rich chocolate, creamy shake and crunchy peppermint candies were almost too much to resist. But, you know what? I held off. You have enough to deal with. Like a naggy wife, demanding elves, and a very stubborn mode of transportation. So you deserve every deliciously boozy sip.

Serves about 2

Ingredients:

- About 3 cups Artic Zero mint chocolate chip frozen dessert
- ¼ cup Patron XO Cafe Dark Cocoa tequila
- ¼ cup low-fat milk
- ¼ teaspoon peppermint extract
- 2 tablespoons chocolate chips
- Crushed peppermint candies for garnish
- Whipped cream for garnish
- Chocolate shavings

Nutritional information per serving:

Calories: 278

Fat: 4.5 grams

Carbohydrates: 35 grams

Protein: 9.5 grams

Fiber: >1 gram

Directions:

1. Place all the ingredients except the candy canes, whipped cream, and chocolate shavings in a blender. Pulse on low until mixture is thick and creamy. Pour into a glass and garnish with whipped cream, crushed candy canes, and chocolate shavings.

STRAWBERRY BALSAMIC MARGARITAS

If you're an absolutely balsamic addict like me, the thought of drinking it isn't strange at all. In fact, it's probably a typical Tuesday night. As much as I love it, the addition of the balsamic to my go-to strawberry margarita recipe was a bit of a fluke, but, oh my lord, did it completely change my life. After one sip I wondered why no one had ever done this before and how this drink could become a permanent fixture to my mouth.

With more than half the sugar of a normal margarita, this is one cocktail you can enjoy without any side orders of guilt (or bloat!).

Serves about 4–5 (ours served 4½)

Ingredients:

- 2 pints fresh strawberries, hulled
- About 5 tablespoons sugar
- 12 ounces premium tequila
- ⅓ cup low-calorie orange juice
- 3 tablespoons margarita mix (we used Drink Skinny original lime)*
- 3–5 tablespoons balsamic vinegar
- About 3 cups of ice

*Sub in more orange juice or fresh lime juice if you don't have that.

> **Nutritional information per margarita:**
>
> Calories: 300
>
> Fat: >1 gram
>
> Carbohydrates: 37 grams
>
> Protein: 1.3 grams
>
> Fiber: 0 grams

Directions:

1. Pour the ice into a blender. Add strawberries, sugar, tequila, margarita mix, fresh orange juice, and balsamic vinegar (start with 3 tablespoons). Blend on low until smooth. Add additional sugar and balsamic vinegar to taste (I added about 4 tablespoons of vinegar to my batch).
2. Dip the tops of your margarita glasses (or mason jars) in water and then roll in crushed sugar or salt. Pour the mixture into the rimmed glasses and enjoy!

SOUTHERN STYLE GIN MIXERS

I will always have a very special place in my heart for Charleston, South Carolina. It's where I spend everything Thanksgiving. It's where I dream of one day owning a home. Oh, and it's kind of where my husband and I got married. Although I have no real answer for what constitutes these gin mixers as southern, it's just a drink that I'd love to have on one of those long, hot, southern summer nights when I'm covered in sticky sweat and being swarmed by mosquitoes but still wouldn't dream of being anywhere else.

Yields 2 cocktails each

Ingredients:

For the grapefruit gin and juice:

- 4 ounces gin
- 6 ounces freshly squeezed grapefruit juice
- Mint leaves
- Dash of sugar (optional for sweetness*)

For the cucumber cocktail:

- 4 ounces gin
- 4 tablespoons fresh lemon juice (about 1½ large lemons)
- ¼ cucumber, thinly sliced
- Splash of tonic water

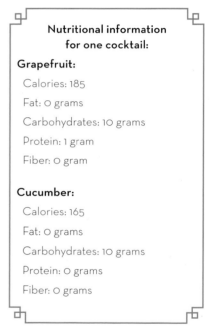

Nutritional information for one cocktail:

Grapefruit:

Calories: 185

Fat: 0 grams

Carbohydrates: 10 grams

Protein: 1 gram

Fiber: 0 gram

Cucumber:

Calories: 165

Fat: 0 grams

Carbohydrates: 10 grams

Protein: 0 grams

Fiber: 0 grams

Directions:

1. To make the grapefruit drink, use a citrus juicer to extract juice from grapefruit. Remove seeds. Pour grapefruit juice into a chilled martini mixer with ice. Add gin and shake. Pour mixture over ice cubes in a chilled glass and garnish with fresh mint.
2. To make the cucumber drink, pour gin, lemon juice, and cucumber slices in a chilled martini mixer with ice. Shake well. Pour mixture into a chilled glass filled with ice and top with tonic water. Stir with a spoon. Garnish with thin slices of lemon and cucumber.

LIGHT NUTELLA EGGNOG

Yes, it's real. Eggnog and Nutella. Together. Intimately. Sharing the same bed. Kissing all the time. Yep. These two saucy little lovers are together at last. And you know what? After how damn delicious a glass of this tastes, I'm going to say they are going to be lovers for a *long, long* time. Each sip of this eggnog is creamy, thick, and full of hazelnut and vanilla flavor. Plus, the addition of the rum gives it an amazing kick of spice. It's like Christmas in a mug, except better since it has less than 10 grams of fat and less than 150 calories than the regular kind.

Serves about 6

Ingredients:

- 1½ cups 1 percent milk
- ¼ cup light cream
- 2 eggs
- 1 egg yolk
- ¼ cup sugar
- 1 tablespoon corn starch or flour
- 1 vanilla bean
- 2 tablespoons of Nutella
- ¼ cup Captain Morgan spiced rum

Nutritional information per serving (about ½ cup):

Calories: 164.5

Fat: 7 grams

Carbohydrates: 10.3 grams

Protein: 5 grams

Fiber: 2 grams

Directions:

1. Heat 1½ cups milk in a medium size saucepan. Cut vanilla bean in half lengthwise and remove seeds. Add the pods and seeds to the milk. Bring to a simmer and let thicken, about 6 minutes.

2. Meanwhile, whisk eggs, egg yolk, sugar, and flour/cornstarch together until fully mixed. Once milk mixture has thickened, add it to the bowl of egg mixture. Carefully whisk them together. Immediately pour the egg/milk mixture back into the saucepan. Let simmer again until thick, stirring constantly until mixture sticks to the back of a spoon or about 6–8 minutes.*

3. Once thickened, remove from the heat and stir in the cream to stop the cooking. Whisk in the Nutella until fully mixed. Place eggnog on an ice bath, whisking constantly, until cooled. **Once chilled, whisk in rum and serve!

*Do not skip the stirring part, otherwise the mixture will congeal.
**Do not skip this part either, or else the mixture will thicken too quickly into a pudding-like substance.

KID FRIENDLY TIP: Omit the rum entirely for a kid-friendly recipe.

DARK CHERRY SANGRIA

The beautiful thing about sangria is how easy it is to make. When you're in a hurry, you can quickly throw in your favorite bottle of wine, juice, and a few handfuls of fresh fruit for the perfect spring or summer cocktail. This gorgeous dark cherry sangria is a breeze to throw together and instantly adds glamour to any table setting or bar.

Serves about 4

Ingredients:

- 1 bottle pinot noir (about 3½ cups)
- 2 cups sweet rose or white zinfandel wine
- Juice from one lemon
- ¼ cup no pulp orange juice
- 1¾ cups low-sugar cherry or cranberry juice
- 1½ cups black cherries, pitted
- 1 orange peel

Nutritional information per serving:

Calories: 246

Fat: 0 grams

Carbohydrates: 19 grams

Protein: >1 gram

Fiber: 0 gram

Directions:

1. Mix all of the ingredients together in a large pitcher. Chill in the fridge for at least an hour (so the fruit soaks in the flavors).
2. Pour into glasses and garnish with cherries and ice.

WHITE WINE SLUSHY

This is the grown up version of those crazy addictive slushies you get at the 7-Eleven. And unlike those slushies, this has real ingredients! Much like sangria, this frozen white wine drink is filled with white wine, chunks of real fruit, and your favorite low-calorie drink. Just beware of brain freezes!

Serves about 6

Ingredients:

- 1 bottle sweet white wine (riesling or pinot)
- 2 cups frozen peaches
- 2 tablespoons honey
- ¼ cup strawberry vodka
- ¼ cup peach juice
- 1 bottle chilled peach wine

Nutritional information per serving:

Calories: 157.6

Fat: 0 grams

Carbohydrates: 15.5 grams

Protein: >1 gram

Fiber: 0 gram

Directions:

1. Place all of the ingredients into a blender and blend on low until smooth and thick. Garnish with fresh strawberries.

SMASHED STRAWBERRY & BLUEBERRY BELLINI

This simple strawberry Bellini takes the normal brunch cocktail up a notch with the addition of smashed strawberries and a dash of fresh blueberries without taking a bunch of time. If you're having your friends over for a last minute brunch, this is the perfect drink to prepare. Your friends will think you're Martha Stewart and you'll get an extra few minutes of sleep.

Serves about 4

Ingredients:

- 1 bottle ultra brut Champagne
- 1 cup strawberries
- ¼ cup simple syrup
- Fresh blueberries for garnish

Nutritional information per serving:

Calories: 193

Fat: 1.25 grams

Carbohydrates: 18.25 grams

Protein: 1 gram

Fiber: 0 grams

Directions:

1. Using a mortar and pestal, mash the strawberries until completely squished.

2. Place mashed berries in a large pitcher and add simple syrup. Slowly pour Champagne into the pitcher. The mashed strawberries will rise to the top. Carefully strain the drink through a wire mesh strainer, saving the mashed strawberries. Pour the liquid back into the pitcher.

3. When making each drink, place about one tablespoon of muddled strawberries into the bottom of each Champagne flute. Pour strained Champagne mixture over.

4. Garnish with fresh blueberries.

ENTICING ENTREES

It only took twenty-seven years, but I finally realize just how lucky I was to have a mom who cooked dinner almost every night. And not just boxed macaroni and cheese or frozen dinners. She would make these incredible meals from simple ingredients like Hungarian goulash with macaroni noodles and ground beef or incredible homemade marinara with super cheesy garlic bread. And then we'd all sit together and eat as a family. When I was a teenager, I never appreciated it. I wished for delivery pizza or takeout Chinese. I loathed setting the table and having to actually sit down and talk to my family. I inhaled my dinner so I could rush back to AOL or my five-hour phone call with my best friend Alaina. I never truly appreciated the meal or what she was trying to do; bring our family closer together.

Family dinners are so important, now more than ever. With our busy schedules, obsessions with social media, and never-ending obligations, a true family dinner is becoming something of the past. A distant memory, a scene you see played out on Modern Family and mumble "no one does that anymore." And that breaks my heart. Even though I didn't participate in the concept of our family dinners, I truly cherish that we did them. In a world of divorce and broken families, I was so lucky to have a unit that was solid, one that sat down and ate dinner together. When E and I decide to have kids, family dinners without television, phones, or iPads will be something we do nightly, not just on rare occasions.

When I was testing recipes for this section, I wanted ones that inspired a family dinner. Ones that would bring everyone together from all parts of the house. Ones that would excite kids and promote healthy, happy discussions. Ones that are not only healthy, low fat, and low-calorie but are also simple to put together and beautiful to look at. Hopefully these recipes will bring your family together the way they did mine.

CHICKEN WITH LEMONY GREEN BEANS

Chicken gets a bad rap. People say it's boring, generic, oh-so-ordinary. To those people, I just say five words. Chicken with lemony green beans. The crispy skinned chicken is marinated in lemon juice and garlic, giving it a punch of zesty garlic flavor. Paired with steamed green beans, this is one healthy main entrée. And it'll turn chicken haters into lovers in no time.

Serves 4

Ingredients:

- 4 chicken thighs, with skin
- 3 cloves garlic, peeled
- Salt and pepper
- 1–2 tablespoons lemon juice*
- 1 tablespoon lemon zest
- 1 pound fresh green beans
- 1 tablespoon garlic salt

Nutritional information per serving:

Calories: 302

Fat: 12.5 grams

Carbohydrates: 12.5 grams

Protein: 17 grams

Fiber: 0 grams

Directions:

1. Preheat oven to 400°F. Grease an oven safe baking dish with cooking spray. Liberally coat a skillet with nonstick cooking spray. Cover both sides of the chicken thighs with salt and pepper.

2. Add chicken and cook on high heat for about 2 minutes or until the skin starts to brown slightly. Reduce heat to medium and cook chicken about 12 minutes longer, 6 minutes on each side.

3. Transfer the chicken to the baking dish. Add garlic, 1 tablespoon lemon juice and cook about 12 more minutes or until chicken is golden brown.

4. To make the green beans, simply bring a large pot of salted water to a boil. Add beans and cook about 6–8 minutes or until soft. Immediately place beans in an ice bath to stop the cooking process. Toss beans with salt, pepper, and lemon zest.

5. Serve chicken with green beans and additional one tablespoon of lemon juice.

* Second tablespoon is totally optional.

CAJUN FISH TACOS

I went to New Orleans with my family when I was in high school. It's funny, I can still smell the crispy, powdered beignets we devoured at Café du Monde and can still taste the incredible Cajun jumbo we had while walking around the art fair. The different spices created a melody in my mouth, the shrimp and fish so fresh I could actually see the fisherman plucking them from the ocean a few miles away. I've been all over the world and to me, NOLA has some of the best food I've ever had. This Cajun fish tacos recipe tastes like New Orleans. The fish is incredibly juicy with the perfect kick in the mouth of Cajun flavoring and spices. If you listen, you can hear the lively jazz music coming from the French quarter with each bite.

Serves about 4 (1 taco each)

Ingredients:

For the tacos:

- Nonstick cooking spray
- 4 (5-ounce) tilapia filets
- 4 soft tortillas
- Salt and pepper
- 2 tablespoons lime juice
- 1 cup packed cilantro leaves
- About 4 capri tomatoes, sliced
- Fresh lettuce or arugula
- 1¾ tablespoons Cajun seasoning

Nutritional information
per serving:

Calories: 292.5

Fat: 14.25 grams

Carbohydrates: 17.75 grams

Protein: 28.2 grams

Fiber: 5 grams

For the sauce:

- 1 cup light cream
- 1 tablespoon flour
- 1 tablespoon unsalted butter
- 1½ tablespoons Cajun seasoning

Directions:

1. To make the fish, evenly coat each filet with salt, pepper, and Cajun seasoning.
2. Spray a pan with nonstick cooking spray. Add fish filets, and cook over medium heat for about 3-4 minutes on each side or until nice and browned.
3. To make the sauce, heat butter in a medium size skillet over medium high heat. Add flour and mix until slightly gummy. Using a whisk, whisk the cream and Cajun seasoning into the flour mixture. Keep whisking until thick.
4. Place each filet in a medium size tortilla over a bed of arugula and sliced tomatoes. Drizzle each taco with about two tablespoons Cajun sauce.

CAPRESE DOUBLE BAKED SPAGHETTI SQUASH

My favorite part of summer is turning everything I eat into caprese. The tomatoes are so juicy they burst when you bite into them, and the basil is growing rampant outside my window. This spaghetti squash has all of the flavors I love in a traditional caprese recipe, only doubled baked to perfection. Besides the flavors, the best part about this recipe is you don't need a dish, just a fork!

Serves 4

Ingredients:

- 1 large spaghetti squash
- 2 tablespoons extra virgin olive oil
- Salt and pepper
- About 1 cup marinara sauce
- 8 ounces fresh mozzarella
- ½ cup fresh basil leaves, chopped
- About ¼ cup freshly grated Parmesan
- 2 medium size capri tomatoes, sliced
- 2 tablespoons crushed red pepper

> ### Nutritional information per serving:
>
> Calories: 302
>
> Fat: 18 grams
>
> Carbohydrates: 24.5 grams
>
> Protein: 15 grams
>
> Fiber: 3 grams

Directions:

1. Preheat oven to 375°F. Grease a roasted pan with nonstick cooking spray.
2. Cut the spaghetti squash in half with a very sharp knife. Using a spoon, scoop the seeds out (careful not to scoop out the "spaghetti" part of the squash).
3. Sprinkle each squash half with olive oil and salt and pepper. Bake for about 40 minutes or until soft. Let cool slightly and then pull the insides of the squash with a fork to loosen the spaghetti squash noodles.
4. Divide sauce in half and pour into the center of each squash half. Top each side with 4 ounces of fresh mozzarella, ¼ cup chopped basil, one slice tomato, and 2 tablespoons Parmesan. Sprinkle with crushed red pepper.
5. Bake again for about 12-15 min or until cheese is fully melted.

SPAGHETTI SQUASH COOKING TIP: Spaghetti squash is harvested in the early fall, so aim to buy the freshest squash around September-November. A tip with roasting: *always* roast flesh side down in a little bit of water to steam the squash and make the "noodles" easier to pull out.

CRISPY TOFU STIR-FRY

When I first started cooking, I was terrified of tofu. The way it oozed liquid and jiggled when you poked it. After a few failed recipes with it, I'd all but given up. Then, tired of the tofu mocking me from the fridge, I decided to conquer it. And this, friends, is the recipe that did it. The tofu is incredibly flavorful with the perfectly crispy outside. Paired with my favorite Asian flavorings, this stir-fry is a regular at my house.

Serves about 4

Ingredients:

- 1 block extra-firm tofu, drained and pressed, chopped
- 2 tablespoons extra virgin olive oil
- 1 onion, chopped
- 2 cloves garlic, chopped
- 5–6 sweet peppers, chopped
- 1½ tablespoons crushed red pepper
- About 2 cups of rice noodles
- 2½ tablespoons reduced sodium soy sauce
- 1½ tablespoons hot pepper paste
- Salt and pepper to taste

Nutritional information per serving:

Calories: 291

Fat: 11 grams

Carbohydrates: 35.5 grams

Protein: 11.5 grams

Fiber: 5 grams

Directions:

1. Remove rice noodles from package and place in hot water. This will loosen them up. Set aside.
2. Heat 1 tablespoon oil in a large nonstick wok on medium high heat. Add onions and cook until softened, about 3 minutes. Add garlic, pepper, and tofu. Cook until tofu is browned and crispy, about 5 minutes.
3. Add pepper flakes and pepper spread and heat another minute longer. Add cooked rice noodles and sodium sauce and heat for another 2 minutes or until mixture is fully combined.
4. Serve with additional crushed red pepper to taste.

BUYING TOFU, WHAT YOU NEED TO KNOW.

If you've ever been to the store, you've probably seen that there is more than one kind of tofu and to a novice cook, it can be overwhelming. Which is why I've put together this little chart to help you know when to use the different types of tofu.

SILKEN: Silken tofu is a very soft, silky, or Japanese-style tofu that has a softer consistency than regular tofu. You'll often see this in boxes without any additional water or refrigeration.

- Silken tofu is often used in baked goods, like cheesecakes, smoothies, milkshakes, or pies.

REGULAR: Regular tofu is the variety that is most often found in the refrigerated section of the grocery store. It comes in three different firmness levels:

- Extra firm or firm: This is the most commonly used type of tofu in stir-fries, bakes, or burgers. Use this when you want the tofu to retain its shape, like in this stir-fry.
- Medium or soft: Use this when you're looking to crumble the tofu in your recipe like when making a mashed tofu or using it like ricotta in lasagnas and pastas.

CHUNKY TURKEY LASAGNA CASSEROLE (CROCK-POT)

It's Judgment Day. The person you've been with on a few sort of awkward first dates has agreed to come over for dinner. One that you're making. The problem? You're not a cook. You burn water, if that's possible. So what do you make? Easy. This Crock-Pot lasagna casserole. The slow-cooker, or big betty, does all your cooking for you, leaving you more time to look effortlessly beautiful or shove yourself into those spanx, whichever takes more time.

Serves about 5–7

Ingredients:

- 1 pound extra lean ground turkey
- 1 can (26 ounces) low-sodium tomato sauce
- 1 can (14½ ounces) fire roasted tomatoes, drained
- 1 can (14½ ounces) petite diced Italian tomatoes, drained
- 4 cloves garlic, peeled and chopped
- ⅔ medium onion, chopped
- 1 bay leaf
- 2½ tablespoons Italian seasoning
- 6 ounces dried lasagna noodles, broken into pieces
- 1 cup fat-free ricotta cheese
- 1 cup mozzarella cheese, part skim, shredded
- ¼ cup shredded Parmesan cheese
- Salt and pepper

Nutritional information
per serving:

Calories: 298

Fat: 5.4 grams

Carbohydrates: 29 grams

Protein: 31 grams

Fiber: 10 grams

Directions:

1. Place all of the ingredients (down to the Italian seasoning) in the basin of a slow cooker. Cook on low for about 6–8 hours, crumbling the turkey and stirring as it heats.
2. Add the noodles and stir them in. Cook for another 1 hour or until noodles are soft. Serve each bowl with a hefty garnish of ricotta, mozzarella, and Parmesan cheese.

STRAWBERRY, PROSCIUTTO & ARUGULA PIZZA

Pizza is one of those sorely misunderstood foods. Many people assume that it's bad for you, full of fat and calories, and has no redeeming nutritional quality whatsoever. Which, given the pizza choices many of us have to choose from, isn't entirely wrong. Before you write off pizza though, can I introduce you to one last slice? This strawberry, prosciutto, and arugula pizza is full of flavor without being full of fat.

Serves about 8

Ingredients:

For the crust:

- 1 package active dry yeast
- 1 cup warm (110°F) water
- 1 teaspoon sugar
- 1 tablespoon extra virgin olive oil
- 1½ cup bread flour
- 1 cup whole wheat flour
- Dash of salt

Nutritional information
per slice:

Calories: 281.5

Fat: 12 grams

Carbohydrates: 32.3 grams

Protein: 11.75 grams

Fiber: 4 grams

For the toppings:

- 1 package strawberries, sliced with leaves removed
- 1 tablespoon olive oil
- 2 cups baby arugula
- ¼ cup crushed walnuts
- 4 thinly sliced pieces of prosciutto, cut into strips
- 6 ounces of soft goat cheese
- Liberal dashes of salt and pepper
- 2 tablespoons oregano

Directions:

1. Preheat oven to 450°F.
2. In a large bowl, mix sugar, yeast, and warm water together. Let sit for about 20 minutes or until it bubbles. Add in flour, olive oil, and salt. Mix well. Let dough sit another 10 minutes.
3. Liberally flour a hard surface. Place dough on floured surface and knead until elastic, about 6-10 minutes. Then, using a floured rolling pin, roll dough out to about ¼ inch thickness. Transfer to a lightly greased pizza pan or stone.
4. Bake for about 8-10 minutes, or until crust is golden brown. While crust is still hot, sprinkle olive oil all over. Add goat cheese and gently push into the warm crust so it melts slightly. Add the arugula. Place the strawberries and prosciutto over the arugula. Sprinkle with salt, walnuts, pepper, and oregano.

TEQUILA MARINATED STEAK WITH CHUNKY SALSA

Let's close our eyes and pretend we're on a sunny beach in Mexico, sipping margaritas in our own private cabana. Hear the sounds of the ocean rolling in, the laughs of other beach goers, taste the zest of the lime in your frozen drink. Now open your eyes. Suddenly you should feel quite inspired to make a dish to bring your mental dream to life. At least that's what happened when I made this tequila-marinated steak with chunky salsa. It's like a beach vacation, but in your mouth.

Serves 4

Ingredients:

For the steak:

- 4 pieces of flank steak (about 1½ pounds total)
- ⅓ white tequila
- 3 tablespoons soy sauce
- ½ bunch cilantro, chopped
- ½ jalapeño, chopped and seeded
- 2 small sweet peppers, chopped
- 1½ tablespoons Mexican seasoning
- Salt and pepper

Nutritional information per serving:

Calories: 262

Fat: 11 grams

Carbohydrates: 4.5 grams

Protein: 25 grams

Fiber: 3.2 grams

For the salsa:

- ½ cucumber, chopped
- 1 medium plum tomato, chopped
- ½ avocado, seeded and chopped
- 1 lime, ½ squeezed, ½ saved for garnish
- Fresh cilantro
- Salt and pepper

Directions:

1. Marinade the steak by whisking the tequila, soy sauce, jalapeño, cilantro, sweet peppers, Mexican seasoning, and salt and pepper. Add steak to the bowl and mix well, making sure the steak is well submerged. Cover with saran wrap and chill for at least 2 hours. (The longer you marinade, the better the taste!)

2. Once steak has marinated, preheat a grill to medium-high. Add the steaks to the grill and cook for about 3-4 minutes on each side for medium-rare.

3. To make the salsa, mix the cucumber, tomato, avocado, lime, cilantro, and salt and pepper. Top each steak with salsa and serve on a platter of chopped cilantro.

EASY WHITE PARCHMENT PAPER FISH

I spent July of 2013 in France. One of the most incredible experiences while there was a hands-on cooking class I took in Bouillac, a town right outside Bordeaux. Although one of the perks was learning from a very cute French chef, I also learned how to cook fish en papillote, or in parchment paper. Now, it's something I do almost weekly. The parchment steams the fish naturally which means less oil or butter is needed in cooking. One of my favorite en papillote recipes is this one, made with flakey white fish and a savory Dijon mayo sauce.

Serves about 2

Ingredients:

- 2 (5-ounce) cod fillets
- 1½ tablespoons olive oil
- ½ cup low-fat or fat-free mayo
- 2 tablespoons Dijon mustard
- Salt and pepper
- Bunch of cilantro

> **Nutritional information per serving:**
>
> Calories: 307
>
> Fat: 18 grams
>
> Carbohydrates: 8.5 grams
>
> Protein: 23.5 grams
>
> Fiber: 2 grams

Directions:

1. Preheat oven to 400°F. Grease the inside of a piece of parchment paper. Mix the mayo, mustard, salt, and pepper together. Add in a few chopped leaves of cilantro.
2. Brush the fillets with olive oil. Rub the fish fillets with half of the sauce and place into the parchment paper. Gather the sides of the parchment paper up, leaving no openings, and tie with twine.
3. Bake for about 15 minutes or until done.

TIP: Cooking your vegetables en papillote is another great way to save a ton of calories in your side dishes. Just make a little pocket as you would with your fish and add a dash of olive oil. Then let steam and have perfectly cooked, low-fat vegetables in no time.

RICH PLUM AND RED WINE GLAZED PORK CHOPS

Plums, which are in season in the peak of summertime, like June or July, are one of my favorite summer fruits. The dark purple skin and sweet, tangy flesh make for a perfectly refreshing snack or addition to a rich sauce, like this red wine base. Pork is a fairly mild meat so the full-flavored plum and red wine sauce compliments it perfectly.

Serves about 4

Ingredients:

For the chops:

- 4 (5-ounce) bone in pork chops
- 2 tablespoons extra virgin olive oil
- Salt and pepper

For the sauce:

- 3 small plums, chopped
- 1 cup dry red wine
- 2 tablespoons honey
- 1 tablespoon balsamic vinegar
- Salt and pepper
- Fresh basil

Nutritional information
per serving:

Calories: 297

Fat: 11.5 grams

Carbohydrates: 19 grams

Protein: 22.5 grams

Fiber: 0 grams

Directions:

1. To make the pork chops, salt and pepper the pork chops liberally. Heat olive oil in a large size Dutch oven. Add the pork chops and cook on medium-high for about 4-6 minutes on each side or until golden brown.
2. To make the sauce, mix the plums, red wine, honey, vinegar, and salt and pepper in a small saucepan. Bring the mixture to a boil and then reduce to a simmer.
3. Let simmer for about 20 minutes or until thick. Add more salt and pepper to taste.

TIP: When choosing your plums, make sure they are fairly firm but not hard. Like many other soft fruits, you want to avoid ones that are bruised or punctured. If your plum is too firm, leave it on your counter for a few days so it can open up and ripen to perfection!

TURKEY BURGERS WITH SUN DRIED TOMATOES AND PESTO

When I'm dieting, a burger is what I miss most. I crave them. I dream about them. I wake up in fits of swear, mumbling about ground Angus steak and chipotle mayo. Which is why I spent months perfecting the perfect turkey burger. It's heart enough that you need two hands to hold and still less than 300 calories. Take that, cow!

Yields about 4 burgers

Ingredients:

For the burgers:

- 1 pound ground turkey breast (lean, 98 percent)
- ¼ cup bread crumbs
- 1½ tablespoons reduced-sodium Worcestershire sauce
- ¼ cup chopped yellow onion
- 1 large egg white
- Salt and pepper
- 4 whole wheat burger buns, split
- 2 ounces fat-free feta cheese

Nutritional information per serving:

Calories: 300

Fat: 14 grams

Carbohydrates: 42 grams

Protein: 12.5 grams

Fiber: 4 grams

For the pesto:

- 1 clove garlic, chopped
- 1¼ cups fresh basil
- 2½ tablespoons extra virgin olive oil
- About 8 sun-dried tomatoes
- 1½ tablespoons walnuts
- Salt and pepper

Directions:

1. To make the burgers, mix the ground turkey, breadcrumbs, Worcestershire sauce, onion, egg white, and salt and pepper with your hands. Form 4 patties with your hands and place on a plate.

2. Meanwhile, heat a grill pan with nonstick cooking spray. Add the burgers and cook for about 4 minutes on each side or until medium well.

3. To make the pesto, place the basil, olive oil, garlic, sun-dried tomatoes, walnuts, and salt and pepper in a food processor. Pulse until thick. You'll have to push the sides down.

4. Preheat oven to 450°F. Add the whole wheat buns to a greased pan and cook until crispy, about 6 minutes.

5. Place a burger on the bottom of the pan. Top each burger with about 1½ tablespoons pesto, fresh arugula, one-tablespoon feta, and the top of the bun.

SWOON-WORTHY SIDES

While everyone else is salivating around the gorgeous golden turkey, I'm silently sneaking bites of green bean casserole or maple glazed sweet potatoes. When Uncle Larry or Dad is carving the prime roast on Christmas Eve, I'm busy whipping potatoes or helping my mom stir the sauerkraut. To me, the side dishes have always been the best part about any holiday meal.

Side dishes are a favorite of mine because they truly make a meal, a meal. I mean, could you imagine Thanksgiving without sweet potato casserole or mashed potatoes? Can you envision that Easter ham without a plate of deviled eggs or a platter of perfectly roasted asparagus? You don't have a dinner party with just a giant pot roast and nothing else, right? I put as much thought into my sides as I do the main course because to me, they are just as, if not more, important.

When creating the perfect skinny sides, I took inspiration in favorites I had growing up. I turned my mom's incredible decadent mashed potatoes into a lighter, fluffier side you can enjoy anytime, not just on holidays. I turned my beloved green bean casserole into something much lighter and healthier with kale and quinoa. Instead of crispy, deep fried French fries, I baked farm fresh green beans into the perfect crunchy side for hamburgers and hotdogs. These are all sides that not only work well next to something else, but also make incredible meals themselves!

CRISPY BAKED GREEN BEAN FRIES

Whenever I'm in the relationship "dog house" I make these crispy baked green bean fries. Aside from murder, these would get me back in his good graces in a matter of seconds. What makes them so good is the crispy crunch you get from baking in a high temperature oven. They're like fries, but so much better.

Serves about 4

Ingredients:

- 20 fresh green beans, ends trimmed
- ⅓ cup all-purpose flour
- 1½ cups Panko breadcrumbs
- 1 egg, beaten
- 2 tablespoons Italian seasoning
- Salt and pepper

Nutritional information per serving (about 8 fries):

Calories: 150

Fat: 6 grams

Carbohydrates: 6 grams

Protein: 2 grams

Fiber: 0 grams

Directions:

1. Preheat oven to 425°F. Grease a baking dish with nonstick cooking spray.
2. In a shallow bowl, whisk the breadcrumbs and seasoning together.
3. Dip each green bean in flour and then into the egg. Then dredge each bean in breadcrumbs until fully coated.
4. Place each bean on the baking sheet and bake for about 4-6 minutes. Flip and then bake another 4 minutes or until both sides are golden brown.

VEGETABLE FRY TIP: You can sub in just about any firm vegetable you'd like to make these fries. I've used eggplant, butternut squash, zucchini, and summer squash in place of green beans. Just be sure to adjust the time cooked as some vegetables cook quicker than others.

RED WINE & CARROT RISOTTO

Risotto is one of my favorite recipes to make. I love that it requires constant attention, vigor, and concentration. I love that you start with these seemingly random ingredients and end up with an incredibly creamy, mouth-watering dish. I also love how you can take it through the seasons just by swapping out ingredients. This red wine and carrot risotto is a beautiful dish to enjoy while the leaves are falling in autumn. It's hearty, without being too filling and makes the perfect pair to your favorite red wine.

Serves about 5

Ingredients:

- 1 cup arborio rice
- 2 tablespoons unsalted butter
- 2 cups low-sodium chicken broth
- 1½ cups low-sodium vegetable broth
- 1 cup chopped onions
- 2 cloves garlic, diced
- 1 cup sliced carrots
- ½ cup dry red wine (like pinot noir)
- ¼ cup chopped fresh herbs
- ½ cup grated Parmesan cheese
- Salt and pepper

Nutritional information per serving (about 8 fries):

Calories: 269.4

Fat: 9 grams

Carbohydrates: 35.5 grams

Protein: 6.8 grams

Fiber: 2 grams

Directions:

1. Mix the broths together.
2. Melt the butter in a saucepan over medium heat. Add onion and carrot and sauté until translucent, about 6 minutes. Add the garlic and heat until fragrant, about 2 minutes. Add the rice and stir just 2 more minutes, or until toasted. Add the wine and heat until it's absorbed, stirring often, for about 4 minutes.
3. Add ¾ cup of broth to the mixture and reduce heat to low. Simmer the mixture for about 4 minutes, stirring constantly. Repeat, adding the broth, ¾ a cup at a time, for about 12–14 minutes, stirring constantly, until mixture is soft and creamy and rice is fully cooked.
4. Stir in the fresh herbs and cheese. Season with salt and pepper and serve.

RISOTTO TIP: Use a wooden spoon to stir the rice as it's less likely to break the grains of the rice than a metal or sharp plastic one.

CREAMY MUSHROOMS

These creamy mushrooms are one of the most perfect dishes. They can either be a delicious side dish to chicken, steak, or fish or can even be used as a sauce over your favorite pasta. Or, you can be like me and simply eat the entire serving for dinner when your husband's working late.

Serves about 4

Ingredients:

- 1 pound baby bella mushrooms, sliced
- ½ pound shiitake mushrooms
- ½ pound cremini mushrooms
- ½ cup yellow onion, chopped
- 2 cloves garlic, peeled and chopped
- 2 tablespoons unsalted butter
- ¼ cup light cream
- ¼ cup nonfat Greek yogurt
- About 3 tablespoons fresh basil, chopped
- Salt and pepper

> **Nutritional information per serving:**
>
> Calories: 126
>
> Fat: 8.75 grams
>
> Carbohydrates: 11 grams
>
> Protein: 8.75 grams
>
> Fiber: 2.3 grams

Directions:

1. Melt the butter in a saucepan over medium-high heat. Add the onions and cook until translucent, about 4 minutes. Add mushrooms to the pan and heat for about 4-6 minutes, or until soft.
2. Whisk the Greek yogurt and cream together in a bowl. Add the cream mixture to the mushrooms and heat for about 3-4 more minutes or until the liquid starts to evaporate.
3. Add salt and pepper to taste. Remove from heat and stir in chopped basil.

SUPER CRISPY KUNG PAO TOFU BITES

I'm a mindless snacker especially when I'm watching trashy TV or one of those ridiculous Lifetime movies. If I'm not careful, I can gobble down an entire bag of popcorn without realizing I did it. That's why I love these super crispy kung pao tofu bites. They have the texture and taste of a pop able snack with the protein and fiber of a main dish. After a few handfuls I'm too full to keep noshing!

Yields about 4 cups

Ingredients:

- 14 ounces extra firm tofu, pressed
- 1 teaspoon Chinese 5-spice powder
- 3 tablespoons low-sodium soy sauce
- ½ cup water
- ½ teaspoon corn starch
- ½ teaspoon crushed red pepper
- 1 tablespoon sesame oil
- Salt and pepper to taste

Nutritional information per serving:

Calories: 158

Fat: 6 grams

Carbohydrates: 6 grams

Protein: 11.25 grams

Fiber: 5 grams

Directions:

1. Preheat oven to 450°F. Grease a baking dish with olive oil.
2. Once tofu has been pressed, cut into slabs and then into bite-size pieces. Coat the pieces in 5-spice, crushed red pepper, and salt and pepper. Mix the soy sauce, water, and cornstarch together.
3. Pour the tofu bites into the greased pan. Pour sauce over to evenly coat the pieces.
4. Bake for about 20 minutes and then stir to flip and bake another 15–20 minutes or until firm. Garnish with fresh greens and enjoy!

LOW-FAT CREAMY ROSEMARY MASHED POTATOES

My mom makes the world's best mashed potatoes. Whenever I'm home for the holidays, I like to watch her prepare them: 2 pounds russet potatoes, a dash of salt, heavy cream and milk, and about 45 sticks of butter, with a big splash of love too, of course. You can taste the melted butter in each creamy, insanely indulgent bite. If calories were no issue, I'd make those every time a craving of creamy comfort food hit. But they are, so instead I make these low-fat creamy rosemary mashed potatoes. Each bite is as deliciously comforting as hers, just without all those pesky calories and fat grams.

Serves about 6

Ingredients:

- 2 pounds (about 6 medium-large) Russet potatoes
- Salt
- 2 tablespoons unsalted butter
- 3 tablespoons fat-free cream cheese
- ⅓ cup skim milk
- ⅔ cup plain 2 percent Greek yogurt
- ⅓ cup Parmesan cheese
- 2-4 tablespoons chopped rosemary
- Salt and pepper to taste

Nutritional information per serving (about ⅔ cup):

Calories: 260

Fat: 5.5 grams

Carbohydrates: 41 grams

Protein: 9.5 grams

Fiber: 2.5 grams

Directions:

1. Bring a large pot of water to a rapid boil. Cut the potatoes into quarters and add to the water. Add some salt so they don't stick to the bottom. Boil potatoes until soft (a fork should pierce right through), or about 8 minutes. Rinse in a colander and place immediately back into the same pot.

2. Add butter, cream cheese, milk, and yogurt. Beat with an electric mixer until creamy. Add salt and pepper to taste. Stir in rosemary (start with two tablespoons and add more to taste) and Parmesan cheese.

3. Serve immediately.

BROWN BUTTER & MUSHROOM ORZO

The answer to the question "gosh, what makes this taste so good?" is simple. It's always butter. The misperception many people have of low-fat cooking is that butter is off-limits. I'm here to squash that by presenting this brown butter and mushroom orzo. It has 4 tablespoons of butter and still has less than 10 grams of fat. Guys, it's time to welcome butter back into your life with hugs and kisses.

Serves about 4

Ingredients:

- 6 ounces dry orzo (yields about 2¼ cups cooked)
- 4 tablespoons unsalted butter
- ¼ cup freshly grated Parmesan
- 1 tablespoon fresh lemon juice
- 1 cup baby bella mushrooms, sliced
- ¼ cup diced onions
- Fresh basil, chopped
- Salt and pepper

Nutritional information per serving:

Calories: 210

Fat: 13 grams

Carbohydrates: 17.5 grams

Protein: 5.28 grams

Fiber: 0 grams

Directions:

1. Bring a large pot of water to a rapid boil. Add orzo and a dash of salt. Reduce heat to medium and cook until softened, about 6–8 minutes. Drain and rinse in cold water.
2. In a 3-quart saucepan, heat the butter over medium heat. Cut the butter into slices and place in the pan. Once butter starts to foam, move it around slightly with a spatula to bring up the bits. The butter will start to brown and release a nutty, almost earthy smell. Once browned, remove from stove and place in a jar.
3. Meanwhile, spray another pan with nonstick cooking spray. Add onions and mushrooms and cook until softened, about 6 minutes. Add salt and pepper for taste.
4. Remove from oven and mix with the orzo. Add the brown butter to the mixture, stirring to combine. Add chopped basil and serve immediately.

BROWN BUTTER TIP: Your delicious brown butter can go from luscious and delicious to burnt and disgusting in a few seconds flat. As soon as the butter starts to smell nutty and aromatic and is the color of caramel, remove it from the heat.

CHEESY KALE, BRUSSELS SPROUT & QUINOA BAKE

If you're new to quinoa, this cheesy kale, Brussels sprout, and quinoa bake is the perfect starter recipe. It's nearly impossible to mess up and has the same taste and texture as your favorite cheesy broccoli rice casserole. Make this ahead of time and reheat for a healthy, simple and delicious weeknight casserole.

Serves about 4-5

Ingredients:

- 1 cup quinoa
- ½ cup chicken broth
- 1 cup water
- 1 tablespoon extra virgin olive oil
- 4 cups loosely packed kale
- 1 cup cooked Brussels sprouts, chopped
- ½ cup low-fat milk
- 1 egg, room temperature
- About 1¾ cups low-fat cheddar cheese
- ¼ cup breadcrumbs
- 2 tablespoons Parmesan cheese
- Salt and pepper to taste

> **Nutritional information per serving:**
> Calories: 286.5
> Fat: 13.5 grams
> Carbohydrates: 26 grams
> Protein: 17.75 grams
> Fiber: 10 grams

Directions:

1. Preheat oven to 350°F. Grease a standard size baking pan with nonstick cooking spray and set aside.
2. Bring the chicken broth and water a boil. Add quinoa, reduce to medium and cook for 15 minutes until quinoa is tender. Add salt and pepper.
3. Meanwhile, heat olive oil in a large skillet. Add kale and cook until wilted, about 2 minutes. Remove from heat.
4. In a large bowl, mix the quinoa, kale, Brussels sprouts, milk, egg, and cheese together. Pour into the prepared baking dish. Top with Parmesan cheese and salt and pepper.
5. Bake for about 25 minutes. Garnish with Parmesan cheese and bake another 3-4 minutes.

GREEK ROASTED CAULIFLOWER

We all have those dishes, the ones we make only for ourselves. The ones we prepare, sneakily, in the kitchen while our spouses play video games or work on their computers. The ones we binge eat as soon as they're done, ensuring we don't have to share. This Greek roasted cauliflower is that dish for me. After one bite, it'll be that dish for you too, I promise.

Serves about 4

Ingredients:

- 1 head of cauliflower, cut into florets
- 1 can of diced tomatoes
- 4 chives, chopped
- ½ block of crumbled feta cheese
- ½ tablespoon of chili powder
- 1 teaspoon of turmeric powder
- 1 teaspoon of mustard seeds
- ½ tablespoon of Greek spices
- 1 tablespoon of olive oil

Nutritional information per serving:

Calories: 150

Fat: 5.7 grams

Carbohydrates: 14 grams

Protein: 5 grams

Fiber: 2 grams

Directions:

1. Preheat oven to 500°F. Grease a jelly roll pan with cooking spray. Spread florets onto the pan and sprinkle with olive oil. Mix mustard seeds, turmeric, Greek spices, chopped chives, and chili powder together. Sprinkle over the cauliflower.

2. Drain tomatoes and add to the cauliflower mixture. Crumble feta cheese over the mixture and bake for about 10 minutes. Add feta cheese and bake another 6-8 minutes or until cheese is bubbly.

CHEESY BRUSSELS SPROUTS GRATIN

I've loved Brussels sprouts for as long as I can remember. In elementary school, I would ask the cafeteria lady for an extra scoop, sans the cheeze whiz, while the other children watched in horror, their mouths agape. I would ask my mom to make them for dinner and eat second helpings (while my brothers used them as mini baseballs to pelt each other with). This cheesy Brussels sprouts gratin highlights my love of these little vegetables. The sprouts are soft and the topping is crispy, cheesy, and crunchy. It's the perfect Thanksgiving or Christmas side dish.

Serves 4

Ingredients:

- About 5 cups of Brussels sprouts, halved
- 2 tablespoons extra virgin olive oil
- ½ medium onion, finely chopped
- 4 cloves garlic, minced
- 2 tablespoons flour
- Dash of salt
- Pepper
- About ⅔ cup low-fat milk or buttermilk
- 1 cup Parmesan cheese
- Homemade croutons or bread crumbs

Nutritional information per serving:

Calories: 300

Fat: 12 grams

Carbohydrates: 25 grams

Protein: 14.5 grams

Fiber: 6 grams

Directions:

1. Preheat oven to 425°F. Place Brussels sprouts on a baking sheet and sprinkle with ½ tablespoon olive oil and salt and pepper. Roast for about 15–22 minutes or until golden brown and soft to the touch. Remove from heat.

2. Meanwhile, make sauce by heating the remaining olive oil in a skillet. Add onions and cook until soft and translucent, about 3 minutes. Add flour, salt, and pepper and heat another minute. Add the milk and bring mixture to a boil. Reduce heat to low and cook until mixture is thick, about 3 more minutes. Remove from heat and stir in cheese.

3. Lightly grease four mini oval cocottes with oil. Layer ½ of the Brussels sprouts on the bottom. Top the sprouts with the sauce. Top the sauce with the rest of the Brussels sprouts. Sprinkle the tops of the Brussels sprouts with breadcrumbs or croutons and additional Parmesan cheese.

4. Turn oven on to broil. Broil Brussels sprouts for about 3–5 minutes or until sauce is bubbly and top is golden.

SPICY CILANTRO RICE

I'm a bit of an herb junkie. Now, before that's taken out of context, let me explain. COOKING HERBS. And my herb of choice is cilantro. This spicy cilantro rice highlights the unique flavor of this pungent herb. The chopped jalapeños and habaneros give each bite a little kick, making it a great side dish to any milder dishes.

Makes 2 cups

Ingredients:

- 2 cups water
- 1 cup rice
- 2 teaspoons lime zest
- 2 tablespoons olive oil
- 1 cup chopped cilantro
- 2 jalapeños, deseeded and halved
- 2 habaneros, deseeded and halved
- 2 tablespoons lime juice
- 3 cloves garlic
- Salt and pepper

> **Nutritional information per ½ cup:**
>
> Calories: 118.5
>
> Fat: 6.5 grams
>
> Carbohydrates: 12.25 grams
>
> Protein: 1 gram
>
> Fiber: 0 grams

Directions:

1. Preheat oven to 400°F. Line a glass baking dish with foil and cover with nonstick cooking spray. Place the jalapeños, habaneros and garlic cloves on the foil. Bake for about 10-15 minutes or until darkened and garlic is fragrant.

2. In a medium saucepan, bring the water to a boil. Add salt and rice and reduce heat to low. Simmer until the rice is soft and tender, about 15-20 minutes. Drain the water and place the rice in a large bowl.

3. In a food processor, add the oil, cilantro, jalapeños, habaneros, garlic, lime zest, lime juice, and salt and pepper. Pulse on low until slightly pureed. Mix the cilantro mixture to the rice and stir to combine. Serve immediately.

NOTE: I'm aware that cilantro is loved by a loud minority. If you're not a fan of the herb, you can swap in another, like Mexican oregano or parsley.

SCRUMPTIOUS SALADS

While many people crave hamburgers, donuts, French fries and ice cream, I crave salads. Giant wooden bowls filled with an assortment of greens, juicy produce, roasted chicken, and shrimp topped with grated Parmesan, stinky blue cheese, and tons of crispy croutons. When I close my eyes and envision the most perfect meal, 98 percent of the time it's a salad. I'm drawn to these beautifully healthy meals the way people are drawn to the fresh baked croissants and beautiful Danishes in bakery windows.

Not all salads are created equal though, and it's important to remember one thing: Just because it's a salad doesn't mean it's healthy, low fat, or good for you. There are many salads that have more fat, calories, sugar, and sodium than a giant fast-food hamburger or four slices of death by chocolate cake. This doesn't mean that a salad has to be boring to be healthy though.

Creating the recipes for this section was one of most challenging. I had to turn my favorite flavors and favorite salads into 300 or less calorie masterpieces; fresh and crispy sides and entrees that could hold their own while still being devilishly light. After hundreds of salads and a few dressing flops, these ten beautiful side and main dish salads were born. There's a salad made with crunchy peanut butter and roasted chicken and one made with shrimp that's topped with a fresh strawberry dressing. There's a salad made with black bean burger patties dressed in a homemade low-fat ranch. And there's a salad that's requested at almost every family event. Whatever your mood, your craving, or your time, there's a salad here for you. Here's hoping I turn everyone into a salad craver just like me!

FRESH STRAWBERRY & SHRIMP SALAD WITH STRAWBERRY VINAIGRETTE

Plum, juicy strawberries are not only the main ingredient in the salad, but also in the dressing too! This offers a double dose of strawberry flavor in a way you never thought possible. The addition of shrimp makes this a great side or entrée.

Serves 4 (dressing yields about 1 cup)

Ingredients:

- 4 cups arugula
- 5 fresh strawberries, hulled and sliced
- ¼ cup crumbled fat-free feta cheese
- ½ medium red onion, chopped
- 8 pieces of fresh shrimp, cooked

For the dressing:

- 8 ounces strawberries (fresh or frozen)
- 2 tablespoons white wine vinegar
- 2½ tablespoons lemon juice
- 1 tablespoon extra virgin olive oil
- Salt and pepper

> **Nutritional information per serving:**
> Calories: 280
> Fat: 12.5 grams
> Carbohydrates: 20 grams
> Protein: 5 grams
> Fiber: 3.5 grams

Directions:

1. To make the dressing, place the strawberries, vinegar, olive oil, lemon juice, and salt and pepper in a blender. Pulse on low until smooth.
2. Mix the arugula, strawberries, goat cheese, and medium red onion together. Top each serving of salad with 2 tablespoons strawberry dressing.

SOBA NOODLE SALAD

With my job, I'm constantly cooking. I make 2-3 recipes a day, and many of these recipes make enough food for 4-6 people. The problem is, it's only my husband and me. And since we'd both like to fit into our clothes (and you know, through doorways), it's hard to eat everything. Except for this salad. We both sat down with an entire bowl (meant for four) and didn't come up for air until it was gone. The soft soba noodles paired with the sweet sesame dressing make this an irresistible side or main dish.

Serves about 4

Ingredients:

- ½ pound soba noodles (about 2 bundles)
- ¼ cup honey
- 3 tablespoons low-sodium soy sauce
- 2 tablespoons sesame oil
- 2 tablespoons rice vinegar
- 1½ cups sliced zucchini
- 1 can (10.5 ounces) diced tomatoes, drained and rinsed
- ¼ cup chopped, diced, or shredded carrots
- Salt and pepper to taste

Nutritional information per serving:

Calories: 209

Fat: 7 grams

Carbohydrates: 34 grams

Protein: 5.25 grams

Fiber: 1 gram

Directions:

1. Bring a pot of water to a rapid boil. Add soba noodles and cook until soft, about 3 to 4 minutes. (NOTE! These cook fast, don't overcook).
2. Meanwhile, whisk the honey, soy sauce, sesame oil, vinegar, and salt and pepper. Mix the noodles, zucchini, and diced tomatoes together. Garnish with the carrots.
3. Drizzle the soba noodles with the dressing and serve immediately.

SANTORINI SALAD

This is my mom's world-famous salad. When I say famous, I mean famous (in our family, at least). It's the most requested dish at any family gathering and it's the one that goes the fastest. Even when there are at least forty other things to eat on the table, everyone gravitates to this incredibly simple, fresh, and incredible salad. What I love most about it is how fresh it is. With only a handful of ingredients, it's as good for you as it is to eat. I promise you, this is the one salad you'll make that everyone will request you make every single time you visit.

Serves about 16

Ingredients:

- 1 box of penne pasta
- 1 container cherry tomatoes
- 1 cucumber, sliced into chunks
- 1 (8oz) container of fat-free feta cheese
- 1 small container fresh dill, chopped
- ¾ cup of extra virgin olive oil
- ¾ cup of white wine vinegar
- Lemon zest
- Dashes of salt

Nutritional information per serving (½ cup):

Calories: 200

Fat: 6.5 grams

Carbohydrates: 43.5 grams

Protein: 8 grams

Fiber: 1 gram

Directions:

1. Bring 6–8 cups of water to boil. Add salt and pasta to boiling water and cook until noodles are soft. Rinse and set aside to cool completely.
2. While pasta is cooling, chop cucumbers, tomatoes, and dill. Once pasta has completely cooled, mix it with the veggies and dill in a large bowl.
3. Sprinkle in the feta and lemon zest and stir to combine. Add salt and pepper to your taste.

TUNA AND KALE PASTA SALAD

If there's one thing you can find in almost anyone's pantry, it's a can of tuna. Tuna is cheap, very low calorie, and more versatile than most people think. Take this tuna and kale pasta salad, for example. It showcases tuna without the need for mayo and adds a much needed punch of protein to this regular pasta side.

Serves about 8-9

Ingredients:

- 8 ounces shell pasta
- 1 package frozen kale, defrosted
- 4 pieces of turkey bacon, cooked and crumbled
- 1 can tuna (in water), drained
- About ½ cup sun dried tomato pesto
- ⅓–½ cup part-skim shredded mozzarella
- Salt and pepper

Nutritional information per serving:

Calories: 302

Fat: 8.1 grams

Carbohydrates: 43.5 grams

Protein: 16.4 grams

Fiber: 4 grams

Directions:

1. Bring a large pot of water to a rapid boil. Add salt and pasta; cook until pasta is al dente, about 8 minutes. Rinse in cold water and set aside.
2. Mix the tuna, kale, mozzarella, and salt and pepper together. Mix the pasta with the sun dried tomato pesto and stir in the tuna and kale mixture.
3. Top with bacon bits and serve immediately.

HONEY ROASTED SUMMER SQUASH SALAD

Last summer, my husband and I lived in an apartment complex. The circumstances for why we were there weren't great, but we did our best to make the best of it. My favorite part of that apartment was the fact it was just two blocks from the city famers market. Every Saturday, you could find me scouring each stall for freshly picked vegetables, warm from the oven breads, and free-range meats. My favorite things to pick up during the summer are squash and zucchini. This simple and light honey roasted squash salad highlights my favorite summer vegetables with just the right bit of sweetness.

Serves 4

Ingredients:

- 2 medium yellow summer squashes
- 2 medium zucchinis
- About 5 tablespoons honey
- 2 teaspoon salt
- 1 teaspoon pepper
- 2 tablespoons olive oil

Nutritional information
per serving:

Calories: 180

Fat: 10 grams

Carbohydrates: 43.5 grams

Protein: 3.25 grams

Fiber: >1 gram

Directions:

1. Preheat oven to 425°F. Line a baking sheet with foil and spray with nonstick cooking spray.
2. Cut squash and zucchini into ½-inch chunks. Place seed side up on the baking sheet. Sprinkle with salt, pepper, and olive oil. Pour honey over squash.
3. Bake for 15 minutes then flip zucchini and squash over. Bake an addition five to ten minutes, or until squash is golden brown. Serve warm.

CHICKEN SALAD STUFFED APPLES

I absolutely love my job. Everyday I have to pinch myself because I'm doing exactly what I always dreamed of. But the one thing I hate about what I do is the dishes. No matter how many times I do them, they always seem to pile back up, leering and taunting me from the sink. That's why, out of pure desperation to save myself from another two hours of dish duty, I've come up with recipes that require just a few. These chicken salad stuffed apples is one of them. All you need to enjoy this low-fat, tangy, and creamy chicken salad is a fork. Because when you're done, you can eat the bowl!

Serves about 4

Ingredients:

- 4 medium red apples
- 2 boneless, skinless chicken breasts, cooked and chopped
- 3 tablespoons nonfat Greek yogurt
- 1 tablespoon fat-free mayonnaise
- 1 yellow sweet pepper, chopped
- 1 celery stalk, chopped
- 1 red sweet pepper, chopped
- About 2-3 tablespoons dried cranberries
- 4 teaspoons blue cheese crumbles
- Salt and pepper to taste
- Cilantro for garnish

Nutritional information per serving:

Calories: 299.5

Fat: 5.5 grams

Carbohydrates: 51 grams

Protein: 26.15 grams

Fiber: 6 grams

Directions:

1. Slice the tops off the apples and scoop out the insides to hollow it. Keep insides for another use.
2. In a medium size bowl, mix the chopped chicken, Greek yogurt, mayo, sweet peppers, celery stalks, dried cranberries (start with 2 tablespoons and add more for preference), and salt and pepper.
3. Using an ice cream scoop, fill each apple with about 3-4 scoops of chicken salad. Top each apple with one teaspoon of blue cheese and a few sprigs of cilantro.

BLUEBERRY CORN SALAD WITH PROSCIUTTO

If there's one food I could eat for the rest of my life and never, ever tire of it, it's prosciutto. In Italy, my family and I ate slice after slice of prosciutto, so thin you could see through it, with fresh hunks of Italian mozzarella and the juiciest tomatoes you could imagine. Now, when I'm craving a taste of Tuscany, I mix up this blueberry corn salad with prosciutto. The bowl is bursting with fresh fruit flavor with the salty surprise of sliced prosciutto.

Serves about 5

Ingredients:

- 5 ears fresh white sweet corn
- 1 cup fresh blueberries
- ½ orange bell pepper, chopped
- 1 large heirloom tomato, chopped
- ¼ cup yellow onion, chopped
- About ½–⅔ cup chopped baby arugula
- 6 slices prosciutto, chopped
- 2 tablespoons freshly squeezed lemon juice
- 2 tablespoons extra virgin olive oil
- 1 tablespoon honey
- Salt and pepper to taste

Nutritional information per serving:

Calories: 205

Fat: 10.2 grams

Carbohydrates: 38.4 grams

Protein: 5.4 grams

Fiber: >1 gram

Directions:

1. Bring a large pot of water to a rapid boil and add a dash of salt. Remove the husks from the corn, clean off the hair, and then place into the boiling water. Let cool completely. Once cool enough to handle, hold the ear vertically and cut the corn from the cobs.
2. Place the corn in a large bowl. Mix with the blueberries, chopped pepper, chopped tomato, onion, and arugula (start with ½ cup and add more if you like the spiciness of the arugula!). Mix to combine. Stir in the prosciutto.
3. Whisk the honey, olive oil, and lemon juice together in a smaller bowl. Toss the salad in the dressing and garnish with salt and pepper.

SPICY BLACK BEAN BURGER SALAD WITH HOMEMADE LOW-FAT RANCH

When I was a senior in high school, I decided to try the whole "no-carb" Atkins diet. I drank Diet Coke, ate only meat and cheese, and lasted all of about . . . six hours. I'm a glorified carb-a-holic. Since a no-carb diet is never going to happen for me, I now watch my intake by limiting my bread intake when I don't need it. When I'm craving a black bean burger, for example, I make this salad instead. These little patties are so loaded with flavor, you won't miss the bun.

Serves about 4 (dressing makes 1 cup)

Ingredients:

For the patties:

- 1½ tablespoons extra virgin olive oil
- 2 cans (14.5 ounces) black beans, drained
- 1 small yellow onion, diced
- 2 cloves garlic, minced
- ½ cup canned corn
- 2 jalapeños, seeded and chopped
- ½ cup chopped cilantro
- 2 tablespoons crushed red pepper
- ⅔ cup breadcrumbs
- 1 tablespoon low-sodium Worcestershire sauce
- Salt and pepper

For the salad:

- 4 cups baby arugula
- 1 cup chopped yellow cherry tomatoes
- ¼ cup shaved Parmesan cheese

For the dressing:

- ⅔ cup low-fat buttermilk
- ⅓ cup fat-free mayonnaise
- ⅓ cup nonfat Greek yogurt
- 1 teaspoon onion powder
- 1 teaspoon chopped chives
- 1 teaspoon chopped dill
- Salt and pepper

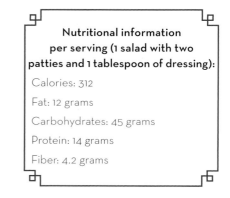

Nutritional information per serving (1 salad with two patties and 1 tablespoon of dressing):

Calories: 312

Fat: 12 grams

Carbohydrates: 45 grams

Protein: 14 grams

Fiber: 4.2 grams

Directions:

1. In a bowl, mash the black beans with a potato masher until soft. Stir in the corn, pepper, onion, garlic, jalapeños, cilantro, crushed red pepper, Worcestershire sauce, and bread-crumbs. Add salt and pepper.

2. Mix the beans with your hands until the mixture comes together. Form about 12 small patties with the mixture and place on a baking sheet.

3. Chill or freeze for about 10 minutes (this will keep the patties together so they don't fall apart when frying).

4. Mix the dressing by whisking the milk, mayo, Greek yogurt, onion powder, chives, dill, and salt and pepper. Place in a sterile jar and chill for about 30 minutes.

5. Meanwhile, heat the olive oil in a nonstick cooking pan. Add the patties, about 3 at a time and cook about 4-6 minutes on each side or until browned.

6. Mix the arugula and cherry tomatoes together. Separate into five bowls. Add two to three patties to each bowl on top of the arugula. Serve with about 1-2 tablespoons of dressing.

PEANUT BUTTER CHICKEN THAI NOODLE SALAD

An important fact about my husband, he's allergic to coconut. So most Thai peanut dressings, curries, and soups are off-limits in my household. That was until I decided to play around in the kitchen and make a rich, Thai inspired peanut sauce without the coconut. The end result was so incredible; I've used it in almost everything. My favorite use, though, is paired with chicken and soba noodles in this slightly spicy, perfectly creamy and zesty Thai noodle salad. It's hearty enough to make a main dish or a perfect accompaniment to sweet Thai curry.

Serves about 4

Ingredients:

For the salad:

- 8 ounces soba noodles (2 cups cooked)
- 2 (6-ounce) boneless, skinless chicken breasts, cooked and shredded
- ½ large yellow bell pepper, chopped
- ½ cup thinly sliced green onion
- ¼ cup chopped yellow onion
- ¼ cup chopped basil
- 4 tablespoons chopped peanuts
- Salt and pepper

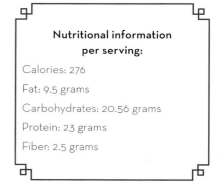

Nutritional information per serving:

Calories: 276

Fat: 9.5 grams

Carbohydrates: 20.56 grams

Protein: 23 grams

Fiber: 2.5 grams

For the dressing:

- ¼ cup low-fat natural peanut butter
- 3 tablespoons rice vinegar
- 1 tablespoon low-sodium soy sauce
- 2 teaspoons Sriracha

Directions:

1. Bring a large pot of water to a boil. Add noodles and cook until soft, about 4-5 minutes. Rinse in cold water.
2. In another bowl, whisk the peanut butter, rice vinegar, soy sauce, and Sriracha.
3. In a large bowl, mix the noodles, chicken shreds, bell pepper, green onion, yellow onion, basil, and salt and pepper. Pour the dressing over the mixture and toss with tongs to combine.
4. Top the mixture with the chopped peanuts.

BEET SALAD WITH GREEK YOGURT DRESSING

You see, friends, I have a thing for beets. If beets were a person I knew in high school, I'd probably have asked them to prom. I'd gaze at them during geometry while I scribbled "Claire & beets forever!" in purple, glittery ink. I love them and I'm not afraid to show it. Which is why this stunning beet salad is an absolutely MUST MAKE of mine. It only has a handful of ingredients but so much earthy, citrusy flavor you could cry. Because beets have a crisp, slightly crunchy texture, you don't need any fatty croutons.

Serves about 2–3

Ingredients:

For the salad:

- 1 bunch medium red beets
- 4 small orange sweet peppers
- About 1 cup loosely packed mixed greens
- About ¼ cup chopped walnuts
- Fresh lemon zest

For the dressing:

- ⅓ cup nonfat Greek yogurt
- 1 tablespoon red wine vinegar
- 1 tablespoon low-fat mayonnaise
- 2 tablespoons Parmesan cheese
- ½ tablespoon lemon juice
- Salt and pepper

**Nutritional information
per serving:**

Calories: 243

Fat: 12 grams

Carbohydrates: 25 grams

Protein: 12 grams

Fiber: 1.2 grams

Directions:

1. Rinse beets with water. Preheat oven to 400°F. Place beets on a lightly greased roasting pan with skin on. Place in the oven and roast for 35–40 minutes or until beets have softened.
2. Let cool. With gloves on (so you don't stain your hands) gently peel away the skin of the beets. Cut into wedges.
3. Slice the peppers thinly so you have pepper rings. Place the lettuce in four bowls or on platters. Top with one pepper's worth of slices. Place about 5–6 beets over the tops.
4. To make the dressing, whisk the Greek yogurt, vinegar, mayo, Parmesan cheese, salt and pepper, and lemon juice.
5. Drizzle dressing over the beets and garnish with chopped nuts, grated Parmesan and lemon zest.

PERFECTLY LIGHT PASTAS

Like many others, one of the first things I learned to cook was spaghetti and meat sauce. In college, when my culinary ability was limited, I would use store bought pasta sauce, dry spaghetti noodles, and ground beef. As I started to learn my way around the kitchen, I started adding chunks of sausage to the sauce or assembling my own meatballs. Then, when I finally felt like a "cook", I made my own marinara with huge chunks of juicy tomato, fresh carrots, and chopped peppers or tablespoons of spices like chili powder and oregano. And then the day my life changed was when I made my own spaghetti noodles from scratch. It's funny, the way my tried and true spaghetti and meat sauce looks now is starkly different than it looked four years ago.

The amazing thing about pasta is that anyone can make them. They don't require many fancy knife skills or grilling expertise. Even if you only know how to boil water, you can make pasta. Truthfully, homemade pasta dough isn't much harder than boiling water. Most require just 3-4 ingredients and can be made in less than twenty minutes. And I promise, once you make your own spaghetti, your dish will take on an entirely new look and feel.

In this section, you'll find my favorite low-fat pasta dishes, from casseroles to sweet potato gnocchi to death by cheesiness mac n' cheeses. Every perfectly light pasta recipe below takes less than thirty minutes to prepare and has less than 300 calories per serving. Yes, even the ultra cheesy baked pumpkin mac n' cheese and the creamy shrimp and avocado spaghetti. Indulging never tasted so skinny!

BAKED PUMPKIN MAC N' CHEESE

A version of this creamy pumpkin baked mac n' cheese was one of the first recipes I ever made for the website I write for. It's been three years and it's still one of the most popular recipes on the site. I've tweaked it a bit to make it a little better for you, but the incredible flavor is still all there.

Serves about 8 (about ⅔ cup serving size)

Ingredients:

- 8 ounces macaroni or shell noodles
- 1 cup canned pumpkin puree
- 1 tablespoon butter
- 1 tablespoon all-purpose flour
- ¾ cup low-fat milk
- ¼ cup light cream
- 4 tablespoons low-fat cream cheese
- ½ cup shredded part-skim cheddar cheese
- ½ cup shredded part-skim mozzarella cheese
- 1 teaspoon pumpkin pie spice
- ⅓ cup Panko breadcrumbs
- ¼ cup shredded Parmesan cheese

> **Nutritional information per serving:**
>
> Calories: 183
> Fat: 5.6 grams
> Carbohydrates: 19.3 grams
> Protein: 8.8 grams
> Fiber: 3.4 grams

Directions:

1. Cook pasta until al dente, about 8 minutes in boiling water. Rinse and set aside.
2. Preheat oven to 350°F. Grease a 2-quart casserole dish.
3. Meanwhile, heat butter in a saucepan over medium heat. Add flour and mix until thick and gummy, about 2 minutes. Gradually add cream, milk, and pumpkin in a saucepan on medium heat until thickened, about 4 minutes.
4. Reduce heat to low and slowly whisk in cheese until completely melted. The sauce will be quite thick.
5. Add in ½ pumpkin pie spice, salt, and pepper. Add pasta and stir it into the pumpkin-cheese sauce and mix until thoroughly combined.
6. Pour mixture into the greased dish. Sprinkle Panko, Parmesan cheese, and rest of the pumpkin pie spice to completely cover the top of the macaroni.
7. Bake for about 20 minutes or until breadcrumbs have browned.

HOMEMADE WHOLE WHEAT TORTELLINI

I never felt more like a culinary badass than the moment I [successfully] made my first batch of tortellini from scratch. There might have been some Rocky music playing, fists thrown in the air, tears shed, and a little celebratory wine drunk. With this foolproof recipe for whole wheat tortellini, you'll start feeling like a culinary BAMF too.

Yields about 2 pounds

Ingredients:

- 1 cup whole wheat flour
- 1 cup all-purpose flour
- 3 eggs
- Sea salt
- Water

For the filling:

- ½ cup low-fat ricotta cheese
- 2½ tablespoons soft goat cheese
- 2 tablespoons chopped fresh basil
- Salt and pepper

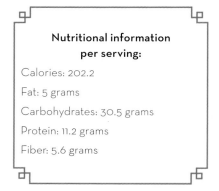

Nutritional information per serving:

Calories: 202.2

Fat: 5 grams

Carbohydrates: 30.5 grams

Protein: 11.2 grams

Fiber: 5.6 grams

Directions:

1. Whisk the flour and salt together in a large mixing bowl. Make a well in the center and add eggs. Carefully mix the eggs into the flour mixture, being sure to scoop the flour from the bottom and sides of the bowl. Using your hands, roll the dough into a ball and place back in the mixing bowl. Cover with foil and let sit for about 30 minutes.

2. Meanwhile, make the filling by mixing the cheese, goat cheese, basil, and salt and pepper. Cover and chill until use.

3. Attach the pasta rolling attachment to the mixer and set to first setting (1). Roll the dough out with a wooden rolling pin. Cut the dough in half and roll out each half as thin as you can. Push the half of the pasta through the roller attachment so it thins out.

4. Repeat another 2 times. Then continue to thin out the pasta by pushing it through each setting until you reach setting 6. You'll want to flour the dough each time you push it through a new setting to ensure it doesn't stick to the rolling attachment. *Don't skip a setting or the pasta won't turn out right.

5. Once rolled out, using a 3-inch circular cookie cutter (or a ¼ cup measure), punch out circle shapes.

6. Once shapes are stamped, fill each circle with about 1 teaspoon of filling. To roll the tortellini, fold each circle into a triangle. Dip your hands in water and press the edges of the triangle together so it sticks. Then carefully bring both edges of the triangle toward each other to make a circle shape.

7. Using the stem of a spoon (or your pinky finger) press it over the top of the round portion of the tortellini.

8. Then press the tips of the tortellini together (so they are stuck) and very carefully pull the tortellini off your finger (or the spoon).

9. Bring a large pot of water to a boil. Add tortellini and salt to the pot and cook until the tortellini float to the top, about 2-3 minutes. Rinse in a colander and enjoy!

HOMEMADE PASTA TIP: Don't rush through your pasta making process. In order for these to turn out, you need a very thin sheet of pasta to begin with. Make sure you run your pasta dough through the smoothing attachment on the lowest level to ensure your product ends out. Skipping this will not only affect the pasta, it'll affect the cooking time too.

ZUCCHINI RIBBON NOODLES WITH PESTO AND PEPITAS

This recipe almost sent me to the ER so it comes with a bit of foreboding. For one, don't use a mandolin WITHOUT the safety doo-dad. You might lose your thumb. And two? Double this recipe if you are cooking for two because you'll end up eating both servings yourself. Zoodles ribbons are the perfect low-calorie, gluten-free substitute for pasta and are absolutely irresistible when paired with homemade pesto.

Serves about 2 (pesto makes 1 cup)

For the zoodles:

- 3 zucchinis
- 2 tablespoons pepitas (or pumpkin seeds)
- 2 tablespoons shredded Parmesan

For the pesto:

- 2 cups fresh basil leaves
- ¼ cup chopped walnuts
- ¼ cup shredded Parmesan cheese
- 2 tablespoons warm water
- 3 tablespoons extra virgin olive oil
- ½ tablespoon lemon juice
- Salt and pepper

> **Nutritional information per serving (½ the zoodles and ¼ cup pesto):**
> Calories: 285.5
> Fat: 20 grams
> Carbohydrates: 13 grams
> Protein: 12 grams
> Fiber: 4.86 grams

Directions:

1. To make the pesto: Place all of the ingredients into a food processor. Pulse on low until smooth.
2. Slice the zucchini in half, lengthwise. Carefully using a mandolin or a potato peeler, carefully peel thin zucchini ribbon noodles. If you're using a mandolin, we set ours to ¹⁄₁₆-inch thickness. If you want more spiral spaghetti like noodles, try a spiralizer.
3. Mix the ribbons with about ¼–⅓ cup of the pesto. Top with one tablespoon of pepitas per serving and one tablespoon of shredded Parmesan.

ZOODLES TIP: BE VERY CAREFUL when using a mandolin! Most come with a safety attachment which will guide the vegetable or fruit over the blade. Not doing this could result in serious injury. If you want super spiral pasta, order a spiralizer. This also works when you make homemade spaghetti too!

SWEET POTATO GNOCCHI

Gnocchi is a small, soft filled Italian dumpling. If you've never had it, stop everything you're doing and make this sweet potato gnocchi now. Before you get anxious about the level of difficulty, let me reassure you, it's one of the easiest pastas to make yourself. One bite of these soft, fleshy little balls of dough and you might never be the same.

Serves about 4

Ingredients:

For the pasta:

- 2 sweet potatoes
- 1 egg
- Dash of salt
- ½ teaspoon pumpkin pie spice
- ⅓ cup freshly grated Parmesan cheese
- ½ cup almond flour
- ¾–1 cup all-purpose flour

> **Nutritional information per serving:**
>
> Calories: 257
>
> Fat: 10.3 grams
>
> Carbohydrates: 31.3 grams
>
> Protein: 11 grams
>
> Fiber: 5 grams

Directions:

1. To make the pasta, heat the potatoes in the microwave until fork tender, or about 5–6 minutes. Remove the potatoes and cool. Once cooled, scoop out the flesh and place into a bowl. Mash the potato with a fork.

2. Add the pumpkin pie spice, Parmesan cheese, almond flour, salt, and all-purpose flour and mix until dough forms. Then, place the dough on a lightly floured surface and knead until smooth and elastic, about 6 minutes. Add additional flour if the dough is still sticky. Then, cut the dough into 4 sections.

3. Roll each section with a floured rolling pin into a long snake-like roll. Then, cut each section into ½–1-inch bite-size sections. Roll a fork over the top to get the ridges.

4. Bring a large pot of salted water to a boil and cook until the gnocchi starts to float. Remove the gnocchi from the cooking water and strain in a colander.

NOTE: Here I added a low-fat alfredo, but you can add whatever sauce you'd like!

EASY ONE-SKILLET LASAGNA

I had no idea just how viral this skillet lasagna would get when I first made it. Truth be told, I was feeling kind of lazy and didn't want to wait for stacked casserole lasagna to bake. On top of this being the most popular recipe on my blog, it's one of my all-time favorites. It takes less than thirty minutes to make and only has 275 calories per serving. Not bad for a lasagna, wouldn't you say?

Ingredients:

- 1½ tablespoons extra virgin olive oil
- 1 large onion, chopped
- 1 cup mushrooms, chopped
- 2 garlic cloves, minced
- 2 (14.5 oz) cans Italian diced tomatoes, drained
- ¼ cup tomato sauce
- 3 basil leaves, chopped
- ¼ teaspoon black pepper
- 1 teaspoon sea salt
- ½ cup skim ricotta cheese
- ½ cup part skim mozzarella cheese
- 3 tablespoons Parmesan cheese
- About 6 ounces lasagna noodles, broken into thirds and fully cooked
- 2 tablespoons parsley (dried or fresh)

Nutritional serving per cup:

Calories: 275

Fat: 6 grams

Carbohydrates: 42 grams

Protein: 15 grams

Fiber: 9 grams

Directions:

1. Heat oil in a large nonstick skillet over medium-high heat. Add onions and cook until softened, about 4 minutes. Add garlic and mushrooms and cook until garlic is fragrant, about one minute. Add in diced tomatoes, tomato sauce, basil, salt, and pepper. Cook mixture until it thickens up a bit, around 5 minutes.
2. Add noodles to skillet and stir into the mixture well. Add scoops of ricotta cheese over the noodles; add in mozzarella and Parmesan. Stir in parsley. Cook about 2 more minutes, or until mixture is thick.
3. Serve immediately with additional basil or parsley.

AVOCADO SPAGHETTI WITH SHRIMP

Sometimes, in this life of mine, I find a gold mine. But instead of stumbling upon gold, I stumble upon creamy, avocado pasta topped with juicy fresh shrimps. This is hands down one of my favorite recipes on my blog. And it came to me after months of desperately trying to create the "perfect" pasta.

Serves about 6

Ingredients:

For the pasta:

- 8 ounces spaghetti noodles
- 1½ avocados, pitted and scooped out of skin
- 2 tablespoons light cream
- 2 tablespoons fat-free milk
- 1 teaspoon sea salt
- 2-3 tablespoons lime juice
- ½ teaspoon black pepper
- 1 cup cooked shrimp, chopped
- 2-3 slices low-sodium turkey bacon, cooked and chopped

Nutritional information per about ⅔ cup serving:

Calories: 283.2

Fat: 15 grams

Carbohydrates: 25.3 grams

Protein: 11 grams

Fiber: 9.3 grams

Directions:

1. In a blender or food processor, place avocados, cream, milk, lime juice, salt, and pepper. Blend until soft and creamy. If mixture is too chunky, add additional milk. Add additional lime juice to taste.
2. In a large bowl, mix shrimp, pasta, and avocado sauce together. Crumble bacon on top and enjoy!

VEGAN HAMBURGER HELPER WITH EGG NOODLES

Even though my mom is one of the most incredible cooks I know, we still sometimes had Kraft Mac N' Cheese or Hamburger Helper for dinner. Not because she wanted to, but because she was raising four monsters (er, children) and was trying to keep the house standing. Now, when I crave cheesy Hamburger Helper, I make this vegan version instead. It's ultra creamy, incredibly cheesy, and filled with ingredients even a six year old can pronounce.

Serves about 8

Ingredients:

- 1 package (14 ounces) Gimme Lean Ground Beef Style
- 2 cups egg noodles
- 2½ cups unsweetened soy milk
- 1½ cups hot water
- 1 tablespoon flour
- 1½ tablespoons chili powder
- ½ teaspoon cumin
- 1 teaspoon garlic powder
- Salt and pepper
- 2 cups Daiya Vegetable Cheddar Shreds
- Fresh herbs for garnish

> **Nutritional information per serving (about ⅔ cup):**
>
> Calories: 300.8
>
> Fat: 11 grams
>
> Carbohydrates: 32 grams
>
> Protein: 16.3 grams
>
> Fiber: 6 grams

Directions:

1. Bread the ground beef protein into a large skillet over medium heat. Using a spatula, crumble into pieces.
2. Stir in the milk, water, flour, crushed red pepper, cumin, garlic powder, salt and pepper. Stir to combine. Add the noodles and carefully mix. Cover the skillet and let mixture simmer for about 6-9 minutes or until mixture is thick.
3. Remove the top and turn off the heat. Stir in the cheddar shreds until melted. Garnish with fresh herbs or salt and pepper.

TIP TO USING GROUND BEEF STYLE: As you'll see in this book, I use it a lot. And that's because it's very low in fat and calories but still loaded with protein and fiber. When using it, be sure to heat and crumble as you would ground beef.

EASY STOVE-TOP MAC N' CHEESE

Every girl, no matter what her culinary ability, needs to know how to do three things in the kitchen. Roast a chicken. Dice vegetables. And make homemade mac n' cheese. Seriously, if you just master the latter, you'll succeed in life. Start with this super easy, oh-so-creamy stove top mac n' cheese. It tastes like the stuff you buy at the store, only, you know, filled with things you can pronounce.

Serves about 4

Ingredients:

- 1¼ cups whole wheat elbow shell noodles
- ½ cup skim milk
- ½ cup fat-free buttermilk
- 2 tablespoons unsalted butter
- 1 tablespoon all-purpose flour
- ¾ cup part-skim cheddar cheese
- ½ cup part-skim mozzarella
- Salt and pepper

Nutritional information per serving:

Calories: 304

Fat: 6.75 grams

Carbohydrates: 34 grams

Protein: 15 grams

Fiber: 9 grams

Directions:

1. Cook pasta according to the package directions. Rinse in cold water and set aside.
2. In a large skillet, melt butter. Stir in all-purpose flour and mix until clumped. Add the milks and whisk until mixture starts to thicken, about 4 minutes. Add salt and pepper.
3. Remove mixture from heat and stir in the cheeses. Pour over the noodles and serve!

BAKED FARFALLE WITH KALE, ASPARAGUS, AND CHEESE

I never have any time to do anything. I guess that comes with the territory of being a full-time writer, recipe developer, world traveler, wife, and dog mother. So when I find a recipe that's both elegant enough for a party and delicious enough for a picky husband, that's a good day. This baked farfalle with kale, asparagus, and cheese is a gorgeous entrée or side dish that's both flavorful and healthy!

Serves about 6–8

Ingredients:

- 10 ounces farfalle pasta
- 2 small yellow onions, chopped
- 2 cloves garlic, diced
- 6 sweet peppers, chopped
- 1 can green beans, drained
- 4 ounces fresh kale
- 1 tablespoon butter
- ¼ cup flour
- 2½ cups 1 percent milk
- ¾ cup part-skim mozzarella
- ¼ cup shredded Parmesan
- ⅔ cup chunky breadcrumbs
- Salt and pepper
- 2 tablespoons Italian seasoning

> **Nutritional information per serving:**
>
> Calories: 302
>
> Fat: 9.8 grams
>
> Carbohydrates: 52.2 grams
>
> Protein: 20.6 grams
>
> Fiber: 5 grams

Directions:

1. Preheat oven to 350°F. Grease a casserole dish with nonstick cooking spray and set aside.
2. Bring a large pot of water to a boil. Add pasta and cook until al dente, about 6 minutes. Rinse and set aside. In another pot of boiling water, add kale until soft, about 3–4 minutes.
3. Meanwhile, melt butter in a pan over medium-high heat. Add onions and garlic and cook until translucent, about 3 minutes. Add flour and cook until a roux forms (it should be thick and pasty). Gradually stir in milk with a whisk, until sauce starts to thicken, about 5 minutes on medium heat. Add salt, pepper, and Italian seasoning to taste.
4. Remove sauce from heat and immediately stir in mozzarella cheese. Mix the sauce with the pasta, green beans, and kale. Pour into the prepared baking dish. Top the pasta with breadcrumbs, Parmesan, and salt and pepper.
5. Bake for about 25 minutes or until cheese is melted.

WHY I'M GAGA FOR KALE!

1. One cup of kale has only 36 calories! Plus it has no fat and 5 grams of fiber.
2. Kale is filled with antioxidants, like carotenoids and flavonoids, which help prevent and naturally fight many types of cancers.
3. Kale is a natural anti-inflammatory food. It works to help ease the inflammation many people face when they fight against arthritis, asthma, and autoimmune diseases.
4. It's versatile! I've used it in everything from smoothies to brownies to cupcakes!
5. It's high in calcium (which is good for bones), high in Vitamin C (which is good for health), and in Vitamin A (which is great for your vision and skin!).
6. It's the perfect detox food. Hungover? Have some kale to help rid your body of those toxins naturally!

ROASTED BEET PASTA WITH GREEK YOGURT

I call this Willy Wonka's version of spaghetti marinara. The stunning purple color is like something you'd see in the chocolate room, where every beautiful piece of nature is entirely edible. Surprisingly enough, the color of this pasta is all natural and comes from the beets! To give each forkful a creamy and tangy flavor, we mixed in Greek yogurt and lemon zest to make it a light, healthy, and totally wild dinner option for any day.

Serves about 5

Ingredients:

- 12 ounces of spaghetti noodles
- 4 large beets, rinsed
- 2 tablespoons extra virgin olive oil
- 1 cup plain Chobani (2 percent is best)
- 2 tablespoons lemon zest
- 2 tablespoons lemon juice
- 2 cloves of garlic, minced
- ½ medium onion, finely chopped
- Liberal dashes of salt and pepper
- 5 basil leaves, finely chopped

> ### Nutritional information
> #### per 1 cup serving:
> Calories: 181
> Fat: 7 grams
> Carbohydrates: 45 grams
> Protein: 8 grams
> Fiber: 3.5 grams

Directions:

1. Cook pasta in boiling water for about 8 minutes or until soft. Rinse and set aside.
2. Rinse beets with water. Preheat oven to 400°F. Place beets on a lightly greased roasting pan with skin on. Place in the oven and roast for 35–40 minutes or until beets have softened.
3. Let cool. With gloves on (so you don't stain your hands) gently peel away the skin of the beets. Place the whole beets into the base of a food processor. Add olive oil, lemon juice, salt, pepper, garlic, and onions. Pulse until it resembles a puree. Add in yogurt, lemon zest, and chopped basil. Puree again until mixture is fully combined. Taste test and add additional salt or lemon zest if need be.
4. Pour mixture over pasta, garnish with extra basil leaves and enjoy!

GREEK YOGURT AS A SUBSTITUTE

Did you know you can use low-fat or nonfat Greek yogurt in place of many of your favorite high-fat creams, condiments, and sauces to cut calories and fat? Here's a quick substitution chart for easy remembering!

1 cup Greek yogurt = 1 cup of mayonnaise

1 cup Greek yogurt = 1 cup sour cream

¾ cup Greek yogurt = 1 cup oil

½ cup Greek yogurt + 4 ounces cream cheese = 8 ounces cream cheese

¼ cup Greek yogurt + ½ cup butter = 1 cup butter

TO DIE FOR DESSERTS

Every year, my mom and her best friend Phyllis make over 2500 Christmas cookies. The crazy part? They knock 75 percent of them out in one weekend. Phyllis drives up from Cleveland with a car stocked with baking goods. I'm talking 5-pound bags of flour, 3-pound bags of sugar and boxes full of chocolate chips in every size and flavor. Her backseat is filled to the brim with decorative trays, mixing bowls, and the most beautiful aqua Kitchen Aid you've ever seen. And in her front seat is enough wine to intoxicate six Italian families. When she arrives, she unloads them into my mom's dining room. Every surface of her six-person table is covered in baking goods. If you aren't careful, you end up tripping over the giant bags of flour. Watching them that weekend is like watching an episode of *Cake Boss* and *The Real Housewives*. They laugh, yell, break dishes, spill flour, knock eggs on the ground, and gossip. Boy, do they gossip. Even though I love helping, threes a crowd in my mom's tiny kitchen. If you want your limbs, you stay out of their way.

One of my favorite parts of this whole cookie extravaganza is when my mom unloads them, giant cooler by giant cooler, into my grandparents house a few days before Christmas. My grandpa, who is diabetic, is obsessed with the little white snowballs she makes, also know as Italian wedding cookies. When no one is watching, he sneaks a few into his mouth, smiling at me from across the table while my mom unloads the bags of cookies. Once the bags are unloaded, she, Phyllis, and I start arranging them onto trays that we put out on Christmas Eve or she gifts as presents. Every year she says she's not going to make as many and then she tops her record from the year before. The joy she gets from baking these cookies is why I started cooking in the first place. I wanted to feel just a fragment of the happiness she feels when she's baking for others.

I will never be the baker my mom is, and I know that. If the goodies I bake turn out half as good as the ones she makes, I've made it. I may not have her skill, but I do have her passion. And every time I bake, I think of her, which always, always makes me smile. So Mom, this part of my book is especially for you. The woman who taught me to love butter and showed me how to make my very first batch of chocolate chip cookies. I hope these recipes, although much lighter than the ones you normally bake, make you proud.

WHOLE WHEAT SUGAR COOKIES

When I was in college, I used to be addicted to Lofthouse sugar cookies. You know, the ones at the store covered in neon frosting and sprinkles that are incredibly soft and fluffy? These whole wheat sugar cookies are my take on those infamous cookies. Lucky for me (and my waistline) they taste just like the store bought variety, just a tad bit healthier.

Yields about 24 cookies

Ingredients:

- 3 tablespoons soft butter
- 2 tablespoons unsweetened applesauce
- ¾ cup white sugar
- 1 egg
- 1 teaspoon vanilla extract
- 1⅔ cups whole wheat flour
- 1 teaspoon baking powder
- ¼ teaspoon salt
- Vanilla buttercream

> **Nutritional information per cookie (without frosting):**
>
> Calories: 66.25
>
> Fat: 3.6 grams
>
> Carbohydrates: 11 grams
>
> Protein: 1.3 grams
>
> Fiber: >1 gram

Directions:

1. In a medium bowl, cream butter and sugar. Add egg and vanilla, mixing well. In another bowl, carefully whisk together flour, baking powder, and salt. Add flour mixture to the creamed butter mixture, one cup at a time, mixing in between additions. *Dough will be crumbly; it'll harden up.

2. Form a dough ball with dough and wrap tightly in plastic wrap or wax paper. Place in refrigerator and chill overnight.

3. Once dough has chilled, preheat oven to 350°F. Line a cookie sheet in foil and liberally spray with cooking spray. Then, on a lightly floured surface, roll out dough to about a ¼-inch thickness. Lightly flour the edges of a circle shaped cookie cutter and stamp out cookies.

4. Place cookies at least one inch apart and bake for 8 to 12 minutes, or until cookies are golden brown. Place on a wire cooling rack and cool completely before frosting.

5. Once cookies have cooled, frost with vanilla buttercream and add sprinkles.

WHOLE WHEAT CHOCOLATE CHIP COOKIE BARS

America's favorite cookie gets a much-needed makeover (and a bit of a face-lift) with this healthy, whole wheat recipe. By adding in unsweetened applesauce in place of most of the butter, you shave off tons of fat and calories. Plus, the applesauce makes the bars extra moist and oh-so-chewy. I heard from a friend (cough, cough) that they pair unbelievably well with your morning cup of coffee.

Serves about 18

Ingredients:

- 2 cups whole wheat flour
- Dash of salt
- 8 tablespoons unsweetened applesauce
- 4 tablespoons unsalted butter
- ½ teaspoon baking soda
- ¾ cup brown sugar
- ⅓ cup white sugar
- 1 large egg
- 1 large egg yolk
- 2 teaspoons vanilla extract
- 1¼ cup dark chocolate chips
- ⅓ cup chopped walnuts
- Melted chocolate for garnish

Nutritional information per bar:

Calories: 213

Fat: 9.8 grams

Carbohydrates: 32 grams

Protein: 3.2 grams

Fiber: 1 gram

Directions:

1. Preheat oven to 325°F. Grease an 8 x 8 baking dish with nonstick cooking spray.
2. Beat the sugar, applesauce, butter, egg, egg yolk, and vanilla together in a stand mixer until creamy.
3. In another bowl, whisk the flour, salt, and baking soda together. Add the flour mixture to the butter mixture and beat. Use a spatula to push the batter on the sides down.
4. Remove from the mixer and stir in chocolate chips and walnuts. Spread mixture into the prepared baking dish and bake for about 25 minutes.

BOOZY APPLE PIES

Apple pie is one of those foods that evoke such a strong feeling of nostalgia for many people. Every time I bite into a slice, I think of the first pie I made with my (now) husband and his mother, the first Thanksgiving we spent together. These mini boozy pies have the same ingredients as the traditional version, just with a little less fat and a bit of booze.

Serves about 8

Ingredients:

For the crust:

- 2 cups all-purpose flour
- ½ cup whole wheat flour
- Dash of salt
- 8 tablespoons unsalted butter
- 6 tablespoons unsweetened applesauce
- About 4 tablespoons ice water

Nutritional information
per slice:

Calories: 364

Fat: 15 grams

Carbohydrates: 49 grams

Protein: 5.4 grams

Fiber: 2.2 grams

For the filling:

- 6 medium apples, sliced
- ⅓ cup brown sugar
- 1 tablespoon apple pie spice
- ½ cup bourbon or vanilla rum
- 2 tablespoons unsalted butter, cut into pieces

Directions:

1. Preheat oven to 325°F.
2. To make the crust, mix the flour and salt together. Using a pastry cutter, cut in the butter until mixture resembles sand. Stir in the applesauce and ice water until mixture forms a dough.
3. Using your hands, press the dough into a disc and cover with saran wrap. Chill for at least 30 minutes. Lightly flour a hard surface and roll the dough out. If you're making one large pie, separate into two balls and roll the dough out to about 10 inches. If you're making mini pies, roll it out to about 3 inches each.
4. Press the crust into a prepared pie plate, being sure to push it up the sides.
5. In a large mixing bowl, mix the apples, brown sugar, apple pie spice, and bourbon. Cover with saran wrap and chill for about 30 minutes to an hour.
6. Pour mixture into the piecrust. Top with a second piecrust and crimp the edges down with a fork. Make slits with your knife in the top of the crust so the apples can breath.
7. Bake for about 45 minutes, or until golden brown. Serve with whipped cream or ice cream!

LEMON PUDDING CUP

These soft, fluffy, and zesty pudding cups are actually more like soufflés or mousse than they are pudding. Instead of being thick or gummy, each bite is light as air. Topped with fresh, juicy strawberries and blueberries, this dessert is almost too pretty to eat (notice I said almost).

Serves 6

Ingredients:

- 2 eggs, separated
- 2 tablespoons melted butter
- ⅓ cup white sugar
- Zest of 1 large lemon
- 3 tablespoons fresh squeezed lemon juice
- 2 tablespoons all-purpose flour
- ¾ cup skim milk
- ¼ cup light cream
- ⅛ teaspoon cream of tartar
- 1 cup raspberries (divided)
- 1 cup blueberries (divided)
- Powdered sugar

> **Nutritional information per serving:**
>
> Calories: 167.5
>
> Fat: 7.7 grams
>
> Carbohydrates: 23.3 grams
>
> Protein: 4 grams
>
> Fiber: 2 grams

Directions:

1. Preheat oven to 350°F. Place ramekins (or mini crocettes) in a 9 x 13 baking dish.

2. Pour egg yolks into a medium bowl. (Set whites aside.) Add sugar and mix until mixture is creamed and thick. Add in butter, flour, skim milk, lemon juice, lemon zest, and cream. Mix until fully combined. (Don't worry, mixture will be soupy looking.)

3. In another bowl, beat egg whites and cream of tartar with a whisk (or electric mixer) until a firm peak forms when you lift up (about 5–7 minutes). Gently stir in about ⅓ the egg whites to the egg yolk mixture.

4. Gently fold in the rest of the egg whites, raspberries, and blueberries until mixed. Pour mixture into each ramekin. Add about 1-inch's worth of hot water into the pan along the side of the ramekins. DO NOT LET WATER GET INTO THE RAMEKINS or your pudding will be ruined. Trust me, I learned this from Bobby Flay.

5. Bake for about 30 minutes or until pudding cake is set and lightly browned. Remove from water and let chill about 30 minutes. Then, garnish with remaining berries and powdered sugar and enjoy!

OREO CHEESECAKE BARS

Sometimes, we just want to eat like we did when we were kids. You remember the days when you weren't worried about fat grams or calories or just how many points were in your favorite dessert. Well, that's why I made these Oreo cheesecake bars. They taste like your favorite childhood cookie while still being light enough to keep you in your favorite skinny jeans.

Yields about 14 bars

Ingredients:

For the crust:

- 18 Oreo cookies
- 2 tablespoons unsweetened applesauce
- 1 tablespoon unsalted melted butter

For the filling:

- 1½ packages (8 ounces each) of light cream cheese
- ⅓ cup 2 percent Chobani
- 3½ tablespoons white sugar
- 1 egg
- ½ teaspoon vanilla
- Dash of salt
- 6–8 Oreos, chopped finely

Nutritional information
per bar:

Calories: 180

Fat: 10.1 grams

Carbohydrates: 18.7 grams

Protein: 5.14 grams

Fiber: 1 gram

Directions:

1. Preheat oven to 325°F. Line an 8 x 8 baking dish with parchment paper with a bit of overhang so you can easily remove the bars.

2. To make the crust, place Oreos in a food processor and pulse until crumbly. (Will resemble sand.) Add in applesauce and butter. Pulse again until mixture is moistened. Using a spatula, press the crust mixture into the parchment paper, being sure to reach the corners. Bake for about 10–12 minutes, or until crust hardens a bit. Set aside.

3. To prepare filling, add cream cheese and yogurt to a large mixing bowl. Beat on high or until mixture is creamy. Slowly beat in sugar, egg, and vanilla. Add salt and beat until mixture is combined. Using a wooden spoon, stir in ¾ of the Oreo cookie mixture. Pour filling over the crust, using another spatula to spread and cover the crust completely.

4. Sprinkle with remaining Oreos and bake for about 35 to 42 minutes, or until firm. Immediately chill for at least 3–4 hours. Cut bars, serve, and enjoy!

PEANUT BUTTER CAKE WITH PEANUT BUTTER ICING

I've never spent anytime in Texas, but I do know one thing, they take their sheet cakes seriously. This dense, soft, moist, and nutty version is my take on the lone star favorite, topped with a so good you'll eat it from the bowl with a spoon peanut butter icing.

Serves about 16

Ingredients:

For the cake:

- 1 cup all-purpose flour
- 1 cup whole wheat flour
- ¾ cup white sugar
- ½ cup brown sugar
- Dash of salt
- ½ teaspoon baking soda
- ¼ cup butter
- ½ cup water
- ½ cup reduced-fat peanut butter
- ½ cup unsweetened applesauce
- 2 organic eggs, beaten
- 1 teaspoon vanilla extract
- ½ cup 1 percent milk

For the icing:

- ¼ cup butter
- 3 tablespoons reduced fat peanut butter
- ¼ cup milk
- About 6-8 ounces powdered sugar
- ½ teaspoon vanilla
- Chopped peanuts for garnish

> **Nutritional information per slice:**
>
> Calories: 255
>
> Fat: 9.5 grams
>
> Carbohydrates: 31.3 grams
>
> Protein: 4.75 grams
>
> Fiber: 5.5 grams

Directions:

1. Preheat oven to 350°F. Grease a 15 x 13 pan with nonstick cooking spray. In a large mixing bowl, mix together the flours, sugars, salt, and baking soda. Set aside.

2. In a medium size saucepan, bring butter, peanut butter, and water to a boil, about 4 minutes. Remove from heat and add to the flour mixture, stir well. Add in applesauce, eggs, vanilla, and milk, stir well.

3. Pour mixture into the prepared cake pan and bake for 25-28 minutes, or until golden brown and a toothpick inserted in the middle comes out dry.

4. While cake cools, prepare frosting by bringing butter, milk, and peanut butter to a boil in the same saucepan (about 4 minutes). Gradually add in powdered sugar until mixture has thickened and is spreadable. Stir in vanilla.

5. Once cake has completely cooled, frost with frosting and garnish with chopped peanuts.

MINI BLACK CHERRY CHEESECAKES

I'm a firm believer that everything is cuter in mini, teeny tiny form. Take these black cherry cheese-cakes, for example. Aren't they just the most precious thing you've ever seen? Just beware of portion control, mini doesn't mean more!

Serves about 12 (½ cheesecake serving size)

Ingredients:

For the crust:

- 1 cup Graham Cracker crumbs
- 3 tablespoons melted butter

For the filling:

- 1 package (8 ounces) cream cheese
- ⅓ cup sugar
- 1 tablespoon lemon juice
- 1 teaspoon vanilla extract
- 1 egg

For the topping:

- 1 pound frozen black cherries (with juices)
- ¼ cup white sugar
- ¼ cup brown sugar
- 2 tablespoons cornstarch
- 2 tablespoons water

Nutritional information per serving:

Calories: 186.8

Fat: 8.7 grams

Carbohydrates: 21.1 grams

Protein: 1 gram

Fiber: >1 gram

Directions:

1. Preheat the oven to 375°F. Combine crumbs and butter until a coarse mixture is formed. Press crumbs into the bottom of a mini cheesecake pan and along the sides of each cavity. Set aside.

2. In a large bowl, beat cream cheese, sugar, lemon juice, egg, and vanilla together with a hand-held mixer until fully combined. Scoop filling into the crusts and fill about ⅔ the way full.

3. Once filled, bake for about 12 minutes or until tops are golden brown and firm. Remove from cavities and let chill in the fridge for at least an hour.

4. While cheesecakes cool, prepare topping by pouring cherries, sugar, and cornstarch in a saucepan over medium-high heat. If mixture doesn't contain much liquid, add water. Bring to a boil and cook for a minute while at a rapid boil. Reduce heat until mixture thickens, about 2 to 4 minutes.

5. Scoop a heaping tablespoon of filling over the cheesecakes and garnish with a bit of powdered sugar.

ROASTED STRAWBERRY ICE CREAM

I have an unhealthy, rather frightening, unexplainable addiction to balsamic vinegar. In fact, when no one is looking (except for my dog, who judges me with all his might), I pour a bit on a spoon and sip it right up. If you're an addict like me, this roasted balsamic strawberry ice cream is going to be your new BFF. It's tangy, sweet, and the perfect balance of rich creaminess.

Serves about 6

Ingredients:

For the strawberries:

- 1½ cups strawberries, washed and hulled
- ½ tablespoon sugar
- 2 tablespoons balsamic vinegar

For the ice cream:

- ¾ cup skim or low-fat milk
- 1½ cups light cream
- ½ cup sugar
- 1 teaspoon vanilla

> **Nutritional information per serving:**
>
> Calories: 202.5
>
> Fat: 12.3 grams
>
> Carbohydrates: 23.2 grams
>
> Protein: 1.8 grams
>
> Fiber: >1 gram

Directions:

1. Preheat oven to 300°F. Place strawberries in a greased baking dish and toss with sugar and balsamic vinegar. Roast for about 15 minutes or until soft. Once cooked, smoosh in a mortar and pestle until smashed.
2. Whisk the milk, heavy cream, sugar, and vanilla together until sugar is dissolved, about 2 minutes. Mix in the smashed strawberries and balsamic drippings. Cover with foil and chill for at least an hour.
3. Once chilled, pour into the freezer basin of an ice cream maker and churn for 15–20 minutes or until thick. Drizzle until done.

SUPER FUDGY AVOCADO COCONUT BROWNIES

Fun fact of the day: An avocado is actually a fruit. Did you know that? Does that make the thought of an avocado brownie a little less bizarre? If that doesn't, one bite into these gooey, rich, and melt in your mouth amazing brownies will make you an avocado brownie believer in no time.

Serves about 14

Ingredients:

- 2 ripe avocados, peeled and pitted
- About 1 cup melted bittersweet chocolate
- ½ cup brown sugar
- ¼ cup honey
- 2 eggs, room temperature
- 1 teaspoon vanilla extract
- ¾ cup whole wheat flour
- ½ teaspoon baking powder
- 2 tablespoons unsalted butter
- 1 tablespoon coconut oil
- ¼ cup unsweetened cocoa powder
- ¼ cup + 2 tablespoons shredded coconut

Nutritional information per brownie:

Calories: 285

Fat: 16 grams

Carbohydrates: 40 grams

Protein: 5.6 grams

Fiber: 2.3 grams

Directions:

1. Mix the avocado, melted chocolate, brown sugar, honey, eggs, vanilla, butter, and coconut oil together in a mixing bowl.
2. In another bowl, whisk the flour, baking powder, cocoa powder, and a dash of salt together. Add the flour into the avocado mixture, stir to combine. Fold in the coconut.
3. Grease an 8 x 8 baking dish with nonstick cooking spray. Pour the batter into the baking dish.
4. Preheat oven to 325°F. Bake for about 28 minutes or until set (you want the middle still nice and fudgy).

BEAUTY TIP: Coconut oil isn't just great for adding a slightly tropical taste to your brownies. Coconut oil is an amazing conditioner (the fatty acids strengthen and soften hair) and works great as lip balm!

WHOLE WHEAT RASPBERRY AND PEAR SHORTCAKES

What's a summer without shortcake? A sad, dreary, unhappy place, that's what. To update this warm-weather staple, I topped each homemade whole wheat shortcake biscuit with the perfect blend of crispy pears and juicy raspberries. And, if we're being honest with each other, a few extra spoonfuls of honey whipped cream too!

Serves about 6

Ingredients:

- 1 cup pastry flour
- 1½ cups whole wheat flour
- 2 teaspoons baking powder
- Dash of salt
- ½ cup low-fat buttermilk
- ¼ cup 1 percent milk
- 5 tablespoons unsweetened applesauce
- 1 teaspoon vanilla
- 3 tablespoons unsalted butter
- 1 egg, room temperature
- 3 tablespoons brown sugar
- 1 pint raspberries, fresh
- 2 medium pears, sliced

For the whipped cream:

- ¾ cup heavy whipping cream
- 3 tablespoons honey
- 1 teaspoon vanilla

Nutritional information
per serving:

Calories: 302.8

Fat: 10 grams

Carbohydrates: 50.1 grams

Protein: 6.8 grams

Fiber: 3.4 grams

Directions:

1. To make the shortcake, whisk the flours, baking powder, and salt together.
2. In a bowl, beat the butter, applesauce, egg, and vanilla together. Stir in the buttermilk and milk. Add the flour mixture to the wet mixture and stir to combine.
3. Preheat oven to 400°F. Grease a baking dish with nonstick cooking spray. Spoon ⅓ cup of batter onto the baking sheet.
4. Bake for about 14 minutes or until golden brown. Cool on a wire cooling rack.
5. Meanwhile, whip the cream, honey, and vanilla together in a mixing bowl.
6. Cut the biscuits in half and top with about 2–3 tablespoons whipped cream, raspberries, and sliced pears.

RECIPE INDEX